DATE DUE		

THE AUTHENTIC LIFE

—OF—

BILLY THE KID

THE NOTED DESPERADO

THE AUTHENTIC LIFE

—OF—

BILLY THE KID

THE NOTED DESPERADO

—BY—

PAT F. GARRETT,

SHERIFF OF LINCOLN COUNTY, N. MEX.

Edited by MAURICE G. FULTON.

INDIAN HEAD BOOKS

New York

This edition published by Indian Head Books,
a division of Barnes & Noble, Inc.

1994 Indian Head Books

ISBN 1-56619-501-2

Printed and bound in the United States of America

M 9 8 7 6 5 4 3 2 1

PREFACE

In refurbishing this early life of Billy the Kid, I have exercised the editorial prerogative as sparingly as possible. The facts of Garrett's account are preserved, although I have made some omissions of what was clearly irrelevant. The style has been clarified and somewhat modernized without, I trust, destroying the vernacular flavor of the original.

The notes appended to the various chapters are my additions to the story. Garrett sometimes was in error and at other times there seemed to be a paucity of detail. In such cases I have felt at liberty to give my own information or conclusions, based on what I have accumulated during a residence of some five years in the section where these events happened.

My obligations for information and assistance of various kinds in putting together this book are too numerous to specify. The most inclusive is to Mrs. R. S. Hamilton, of Roswell, New Mexico, through whose kindness I obtained a copy of Garrett's book used as the basis of this revision. This copy would have gone its way into the limbo of disapproved books if it had not been that her husband, the late R. S. Hamil-

Preface

ton, had more of antiquarian inclinations than most of
the early settlers and so appreciated the value of the
contemporary records of the frontier.

M. G. F.

Roswell, New Mexico,
September, 1927.

CONTENTS

vii

Contents

Contents

ILLUSTRATIONS

FOREWORD BY THE EDITOR

The Book

"A faithful and interesting narrative"—this was the terse commendation of itself on the title-page of the paper-backed volume, locally printed at Santa Fe in 1882, which nowadays those who know in any way of its existence commonly call "Pat Garrett's Life of the Kid." Even forty-five years after the event this description epitomizes the claim the book may have on later readers. Such persons as may prefer "fanciless fact" to melodramatic fiction when they read about the characters of the epic days of the Old West will turn with zest to this contemporary account of Billy the Kid, the young desperado of the South-west who has so mightily caught and held the popular imagination that present-day writers are brisk in producing articles and books to supply the demand for accounts of his deeds.

Garrett's book originated as a counteractive to the earlier accounts of the Kid, which from the start displayed a tendency to take on the tone of the penny dreadful. Although Garrett may sometimes err in a point of detail or in an interpretation of a set of circumstances, nevertheless the impression made by his book is that it contains first-hand history, presented simply, vividly, modestly. At any rate, the information in the book coincides in the main with the body of truth regarding the Kid which has emerged ultimately out of the welter of confused and divided opinion concerning him existing at the time of his death. Garrett was not a man given to exaggeration or misrepresentation and this is a strong credential for the faithfulness of his account. When Garrett states, as he does in the introduction to the book, that in compiling the material found in it he has been at pains to learn the true facts about the Kid, this statement may be taken at its face value.

Among Garrett's acquaintances it is generally understood that in the preparation of the book he availed himself of the assistance of M. A. Upson, generally known in New Mexico as Ash Upson. The latter was a former newspaper man living at the time in Garrett's house and serving him in the capacity of a secretary. Previously in his migratory career in the Territory Upson had worked for newspapers in Santa Fe and in Silver City, and while in both places had been an inmate of boarding houses kept by Mrs. Antrim, the Kid's mother. Thus he had known the Kid in his boyhood and could furnish definite details about this period in his life. It must be admitted that some of the earlier incidents are highly colored, but this is probably attributable not so much to distortion of facts as to adopting that floridity of style which a newspaper writer of Upson's type would think needful in order to give a proper literary flavor. Even in such parts of the book the substratum of "pure, crude fact" is clearly discernible.

When the account reaches the period of Garrett's own acquaintance with the Kid, and especially when it comes to the details of the pursuit of the young outlaw, then the book loses all over-coloring and turgidity and becomes a matter-of-fact chronicle of a memorable man-hunt by the man who planned and consummated it. Garrett and the Kid became acquainted at Fort Sumner in or about the year 1879, and there was such a continued association between them that possibly it should be termed a friendship. In this way Garrett came to know the Kid for what he was and was able to give even the desperado his dues in the book. Taken as a whole it is a fair and sympathetic portrayal of the Kid.

Billy the Kid

It is no murderous, super-outlaw that Garrett's book presents as the protagonist in this episode of the suppression of lawlessness in that section of the frontier in regard to which there was the common saying "No law beyond the Pecos." Garrett knew that the Kid was no killer in the sense of slaying for the pure joy of slaying when once his anger or some other cause seemed to decree that a man must die. He also appreciated the fact that the Kid but showed the mettle of his pasture, which was the lawless and brutal frontier, and fairly should be considered the natural product of its conditions and ideals.

The Kid is first shown as a high-spirited lad growing up in the wild and hard environment of mining camps and at a comparatively early age getting himself into a scrape which, combined with the fact that he was not altogether happy in his home surroundings, resulted in his getting adrift from what there had been of better influences in his life. Then followed a series of adventures with Mexicans and Indians such as were not impossible in those times to adventurous and madcap youth. Eventually there came contact with the winning personality of the young Englishman, Tunstall, out of which there developed a strong mutual liking between these two—Tunstall a product of England's older civilization and refinement, and the Kid a product of the un-civilization of the West and its rough, turbulent life.

Billy the Kid

The brutal murder of this new-found friend aroused in the Kid all the desire for vengeance a lad of eighteen could feel who had grown up in a section whose code was oftentimes the elemental and direct one of an eye for an eye and a life for a life. In a few months, he had killed, or to be more exact, had participated in the killing of several who had been among the conspicuous figures in the killing of Tunstall, and because of this zeal for vengeance together with a native capacity for leadership, had become the outstanding figure in the feud that then existed in Lincoln County between the sympathizers of Tunstall and his partner, McSween, and the adherents of the rival faction controlled by Murphy, Dolan, and Riley.

With the subsidence of this feud, the Kid had along with others on both sides the opportunity to avail himself of the amnesty offered by Governor Wallace and become a law-abiding citizen. But having no confidence in the ability of the law to give at that time either justice or protection, the Kid elected to become an outlaw in the full sense of the word, earning his living by dealing monte and stealing cattle. From this time to the end of his career his outlawry consisted not of murdering but of marauding expeditions, the booty of which was the loosely-owned cattle that grazed upon the wide ranges of eastern New Mexico and the Texas

Panhandle. The Kid's crew was not the only one engaged in this lawless occupation, and, in fact, it did not cause the cattlemen of the Panhandle as much trouble as some others, but those were times when a man might murder his fellow-man and get away with it with more ease than he might steal his neighbor's cow or horse, and so the Kid's exasperating depredations brought forth a decree that they must be terminated. The cattlemen sent into New Mexico their representatives, first Stewart and then Poe, with orders to stay on the job and spare no expense until the Kid and his band were suppressed. Joining forces with Garrett, then sheriff of Lincoln County, they were soon dogging the Kid in a relentless pursuit that did not abate until his capture.

One of the things that made the Kid stand out from the other killers and cattle thieves that infested the land was his spectacular escape from custody in Lincoln. More than any other one thing in his career that display of cool daring caught popular imagination and served to immortalize the Kid when others of his kind have been forgotten. A few months later there came an almost equally spectacular "last scene of all" for the Kid, when Garrett shot him in the dark of Pete Maxwell's room, and the Kid found his place in the pantheon of frontier figures.

Popular sympathy has always strongly favored the

Billy the Kid

Kid. When practically every one prominent in the Lincoln County troubles—and some were guilty of as grave crimes even in the way of murder as the Kid ever committed—received amnesty, it does look as though he were made the scapegoat in that outbreak of disorder. There are those in the South-west who do not hesitate to say that there was a certain powerful man of that section who could have secured for the Kid a pardon but that this man had wronged the Kid to such a degree that he felt safer with the Kid either behind prison bars or in his grave.

One of the perennial questions in connection with the Kid is, how many men did he kill? On this point there will in all likelihood be continued disagreement, but it is safe to find in the traditional total of "twenty-one, not counting Mexicans and Indians," the exaggeration usual in the holocausts of Western gun-men. If such a total ever came from the Kid's own lips, it must have been born in some moment of thrasonical brag, a quality of which he was not perhaps entirely free. According to Emerson Hough, who talked the matter over fully with Garrett in later days, the Kid had killed eleven or twelve men, and that is a more believable tally. In Garrett's book, there are apparently twelve American victims of the Kid's weapons. But by far the majority of this number were killed in affrays in which other Winchesters and six-shooters than those of the Kid dealt death. Such were the circumstances when Morton and Baker and Hindman and Brady and Buckshot Roberts and Bernstein and Bob Beckwith and Carlyle were killed. If these be subtracted from the list, then his own weapons seem to be responsible for five killings—the ruffian at Silver City who spoke insultingly of his mother, the soldier blacksmith at Fort Bowie, the Texas bully, Grant, at Fort Sumner, and the two guards, Bell and Ollinger, killed in the escape from jail the last time. As for the Mexicans, there were probably a few during the time the Kid was in Mexico, but generally the Kid was on good terms with the Mexican population in New Mexico, which either feared or respected him too much to give him cause for killings. In the case of Indian victims, there probably were many, for in those times opportunities for a rather wholesale slaughter of Indians were easy to find. Rather diligent inquiry has failed to reveal any other killings either among Americans, Mexicans, or Indians than those given in Garrett's book.

Pat Garrett

Although primarily a picture of the Kid, Garrett's book does not fail to give an idea of Garrett himself, the man who was the antagonist in this episode. When those of the settlers in Lincoln County who desired law and order for that distracted section felt strong enough to assert themselves, they had Garrett made sheriff. For a few years before this Garrett had been living at Fort Sumner, having come hither from Alabama by way first of Louisiana and then of the buffalo-inhabited plains of western Texas. But he had eventually made a change of residence from Fort Sumner, then in San Miguel County, to the vicinity of Roswell, then in Lincoln County. The law-abiding element now seeking to curtail the activities of the Kid and others as bad or even worse, knew that they could not work effectively through outsiders, and therefore they determined to choose as their agent one who was familiar with the ways of the men they wished to suppress and with their haunts. Garrett seemed to be the man for the job, and the results showed that confidence in him was not misplaced.

Garrett went at his task with energy and determination, undeterred by any of his former sympathies and associations. During the several preceding years, the lawlessness of Lincoln County had taken on such a grim character that it had been dubbed rightly war and should be viewed from that angle. The killing of Brady, to speak of but one example, indefensible from the view-point of peace times which never sanctions the ambuscade, might become, from the angle of warfare, fine strategy, good generalship, or something of the kind. So in bringing to a close this period of lawlessness, Garrett as sheriff adopted methods that were orthodox enough from the view-point of war. In the light of all the conditions it seems captious fault-finding to say that Garrett should have gone about his difficult and dangerous task with the punctilio incident to an affair of honor.

Garrett was never harsh or vindictive in his capturing or handling of law-breakers, and it is a misrepresentation to show him, as some accounts have done, with such traits. With the Kid, he endeavored to persuade him to change his ways and leave the country, but the Kid would not accept the advice of his former friend. So there was no other course for Garrett, who was always courageous and relentless in pursuit, except to follow the Kid until he had him in the toils. It is frankly to be doubted whether the Kid at Stinking Spring would have ever surrendered himself and his companions to any one except Garrett. The Kid knew that if Garrett gave a promise that their lives would be protected that promise would be kept and the incident at Las Vegas in standing off the blustering mob is one that leaves a pleasant savour in the mind both with respect to captor and captured.

Garrett's ultimate killing of the Kid was undesigned and virtually obligatory under the instinct of self-protection. Garrett would beyond question have preferred to re-capture the Kid, but the two met the last time under circumstances that made it impossible for either to use the amenities of the duello. The Kid happened to be the one to hesitate, and Garrett took advantage of that hesitation. Perhaps partisans of the Kid should be satisfied to have the end come from Garrett's revolver rather than from the hangman's noose. At any rate, Garrett emerges from the turbulence and disorder of those times as the one who undertook a certain job in behalf of law and order and who succeeded in accomplishing his task. And so he too finds a place in a pantheon, the pantheon of those sheriffs and marshals and other officers of the law in the Old West who went forth valiantly to ride, to shoot, and, if need be, to die in their efforts to bring in the reign of law over what was at one time literally the Wild West.

MAURICE GARLAND FULTON.

THE AUTHENTIC LIFE

— OF —

BILLY THE KID,

THE NOTED DESPERADO
OF THE SOUTHWEST,

WHOSE DEEDS OF DARING AND BLOOD HAVE
MADE HIS NAME A TERROR IN

NEW MEXICO,
ARIZONA & NORTHERN MEXICO.

— BY —

PAT F. GARRETT,

SHERIFF OF LINCOLN COUNTY, N. MEX.

BY WHOM

HE WAS FINALLY HUNTED DOWN &
CAPTURED BY KILLING HIM.

☞A FAITHFUL, INTERESTING NARRATIVE☜

SANTA FE, NEW MEXICO:

NEW MEXICO PRINTING & PUBLISHING CO.,

—— 1882 ——

INTRODUCTORY

Yielding to repeated solicitations from various sources, I have undertaken the task of compiling for publication a true history of the life, adventures, and tragic death of William H. Bonney, better known as Billy the Kid, whose daring deeds and bloody crimes have excited, during recent years, the wonder of one-half the world, and the admiration or detestation of the other half.

I am incited to this labor in a measure by an impulse to correct the thousand false statements which have appeared in the newspapers and in yellow-covered cheap novels. Of the latter no less than three have been foisted upon the public, any one of which might have been the history of any other outlaw who ever lived, but which was miles from correct as applied to the Kid. These pretend to disclose his name, the place of his nativity, the particulars of his career, the circumstances which drove him to his desperate life, detailing a hundred deeds of reckless crime of which he was never guilty and in localities which he never visited. I would dissever the Kid's memory from that of meaner villains whose deeds have been attributed to him. I will strive to do justice to his character, give him credit for all the virtues he possessed—and he was by no means devoid of virtues—but shall not spare deserved opprobrium for his heinous offenses against humanity and the laws.

I have known the Kid personally since and during the continuance of what is known as the Lincoln County War, up to the moment of his death, of which I was the unfortunate instrument in the discharge of my official duty. At camp-fires, on the trail, on the prairies, and at many different plazas, I have listened to his disconnected recital of events in his early and his more recent life. In gathering correct information, I have interviewed many persons since the Kid's death with whom he was intimate and to whom he conversed freely of his affairs. I am in daily intercourse with one of his friends who was a boarder at the house of the Kid's mother at Silver City, New Mexico, in 1873. This man has known Bonney well from that time to his death and has traced his career carefully and not with indifference. I have communicated by letter with various reliable parties in New York, Kansas, Colorado, New Mexico, Arizona, Texas, Chihuahua, Sonora, and other states of Mexico in order to catch up any missing links in his life, and I can safely guarantee that the reader will find in my book a true and concise account of the principal interesting events therein, without exaggeration or excusation.

I make no pretensions of literary ability, but propose to give to the public in intelligible English "a round, unvarnished tale," unadorned with superfluous verbiage. The truth, in the life of young Bonney, needs no pen dripped in blood to thrill the heart and stay its pulsations. Under the *nom de guerre* of the Kid his most bloody and desperate deeds were done—a name which will live in the annals of daring crime so long as those of Dick Turpin and Claude Duval shall be remembered. This verified history of the Kid's exploits, with all the exaggeration removed, will exhibit him as the peer of any fabled brigand on record, unequalled in desperate courage, presence of mind in danger, devotion to his allies, generosity to his foes, gallantry, and all the elements which appeal to the holier emotions, while those readers who would revel in pictured scenes of slaughter may batten until their morbid appetites are surfeited on bloody frays and mortal encounters, unaided by fancy or the pen of fiction.

The Kid's career of crime was not the outgrowth of an evil disposition, nor was it caused by unchecked youthful indiscretions. It was the result of untoward, in fact unfortunate, circumstances, acting upon a bold, reckless, ungoverned and ungovernable spirit, which no physical restraint could check, no danger appal, and no power less potent than death could conquer. The Kid had a lurking devil in him. It was a good-humored jovial imp, or a cruel and bloodthirsty fiend, as circumstances prompted. Circumstances favored the worser angel, and the Kid fell.

A dozen affidavits have been offered me for publication in verification of the truth of my work. I have refused them all with thanks. Let those doubt who will.

PAT F. GARRETT.

Roswell, New Mexico,
    1882.

THE AUTHENTIC LIFE

—OF—

BILLY THE KID

THE NOTED DESPERADO

PAT GARRETT

Pat Garrett (1850-1908) was a renowned peace officer of the old West. Though most widely known for delivering eastern New Mexico from the menace and demoralization of Billy the Kid, Garrett on many other occasions rendered signal service as a defender of law and order while at different periods of his life acting as sheriff of Lincoln County, New Mexico, as a commander of rangers in Wheeler County, Texas, and as sheriff of Dona Anna County, New Mexico.

THE AUTHENTIC LIFE OF
BILLY THE KID

CHAPTER I

Childhood and Youth—Sudden and Quick in Quarrel Even in Boyhood—Always a Defender of the Helpless—High Regard for
His Mother—His First Murder.

WILLIAM H. BONNEY, the hero of this history, was
born in the city of New York, November 23, 1859.
But little is known of his father, for he died when
Billy was very young, and the son had little recollection
of his father. In 1862, the family, consisting of the
father, mother, and two boys, of whom Billy was the
elder, emigrated to Coffeyville, Kansas. Soon after
settling there, the father died; and the mother, with
her two boys, removed to Colorado, where she married a man named Antrim, who is said to be living now
[1882] at or near Georgetown, in Grant County, New
Mexico, and is the only survivor of the family of four
which removed to Santa Fe, New Mexico, shortly after
the marriage. Billy was then four or five years of age.
These facts are about all that can be gleaned of Billy's
early childhood.

The Authentic Life of

Antrim remained at or near Santa Fe for some years, or until Billy was about eight years of age. It was here that the boy began to exhibit that spirit of reckless daring, joined to a generous and tender feeling which rendered him the darling of his young companions in his gentler moods and their terror when the angry fit was on him. It was here that he became adept at cards and noted among his comrades as successfully aping the genteel vices of his elders. It has been said that at this tender age he was convicted of larceny in Santa Fe, but as a careful examination of the court records of that city fails to support the rumor, and as Billy, during all his after life, was never charged with a little meanness or petty crime, the statement is to be doubted.

About the year 1868, when Billy was eight or nine years of age, Antrim again moved and took up his residence at Silver City, in Grant County, New Mexico. From this date to 1871, or until Billy was twelve years old, the boy exhibited no characteristics prophesying his desperate and disastrous future. Bold, daring, and reckless, he was open-handed, generous-hearted, frank, and manly. He was a favorite with all classes and ages; especially was he loved and admired by the old and decrepit and the young and helpless. To such he was a champion, a defender, a benefactor, a right arm.

Billy the Kid

He was never seen to address a lady, especially an elderly one, but with his hat in his hand; and did her attire or appearance evidence poverty, it was a poem to see the eager, sympathetic, compassionate look in Billy's sunny face, as he proffered assistance or afforded information. A little child never lacked a lift across a gutter or the assistance of a strong arm to carry a heavy burden when Billy was in sight.

To those who knew his mother, his courteous, kindly, and benevolent spirit was no mystery. She was evidently of Irish descent. Her husband called her Kathleen. She was about medium height, straight and graceful in form, with regular features, light blue eyes, and luxuriant golden hair. She was not a beauty, but what the world calls a fine-looking woman. She kept boarders in Silver City, and her charity and goodness of heart were proverbial. Many a hungry tenderfoot has had cause to bless the fortune which led him to her door. In all her deportment she exhibited the unmistakable characteristics of a lady—a lady by instinct and education.

Billy loved his mother. He loved and honored her more than anything else on earth. Yet his home was not a happy one to him. He has often declared that the tyranny and cruelty of his stepfather drove him from home and a mother's influence, and that Antrim was responsible for his going to the bad. However this may be, it is very certain that, after the death of his mother some four years since, the stepfather would have been unfortunate had he come in contact with his elder stepson.

Billy's educational advantages were limited, as were those of all the youth of this border country. He attended public school, but acquired more information at his mother's knee than from the village pedagogue. With great natural intelligence and an active brain, he became a fair scholar. He wrote a fair letter, was a tolerable arithmetician, but beyond this he did not aspire.

The best and brightest side of Billy's character has been portrayed above. The shield had another side never exhibited to his best friends or to the weak and the helpless. His temper was fearful, and in his angry moods he was dangerous. He was not loud or swaggering or boisterous. He never threatened. He had no bark; or if he did, the bite came first. He never took advantage of an antagonist; but, barring size and weight, would, when aggrieved, fight any man in Silver City. His misfortune was that he could not and would not stay whipped. When over-sized and worsted in a fight, he sought such arms as he could buy, borrow, beg, or steal, and used them upon more than one occasion with murderous intent.

During the latter portion of Billy's residence in Silver City, he was the constant companion of Jesse Evans, a mere boy but as daring and dangerous as many an older and more experienced desperado. He was older than Billy and constituted himself a sort of preceptor to our hero. These two were destined to participate jointly in many dangerous adventures, many narrow escapes, and several bloody affrays in the next few years; and fast friends as they now were, the time was soon to come when they would be arrayed in opposition to each other, each thirsting for the other's blood and neither shrinking from the conflict. They parted for the time being at Silver City, but they met many times during Billy's short and bloody career.

When young Bonney was about twelve years of age, he first imbrued his hand in human blood. This affair, it may be said, was the turning point in his life, for it outlawed him and left him a victim to his worser impulses and passions. As Billy's mother was passing a knot of idlers on the street, one of the loafers made an insulting remark about her. Billy heard it, and quick as thought, with blazing eyes, he planted a stinging blow on the blackguard's mouth. Then springing out into the middle of the street, he stooped for a rock.

The brute made a rush for the boy, but as he passed Ed Moulton, a well-known citizen of Silver City, he received a stunning blow on the ear which felled him, while Billy was caught and restrained. However, the punishment inflicted on the offender by no means satisfied Billy. Burning for revenge, he visited a miner's cabin, procured a Sharp's rifle, and started in search of his intended victim. By good fortune, Moulton saw him with the gun, and with some difficulty persuaded him to return it.

Some three weeks subsequent to this adventure, Moulton, who was a wonderfully powerful and active man, skilled in the art of self-defense and with something of the prize-fighter in his composition, became involved in a rough-and-tumble bar-room fight at Joe Dyer's saloon. He had two "shoulder-strikers" to contend with and was getting the best of both of them, when Billy's antipathy—the man who had been the recipient of one of Moulton's "lifters"—who was standing by, thought he saw an opportunity to take cowardly revenge on Moulton, and rushed upon him with a heavy bar-room chair upraised.

Billy was usually a spectator, when not a principal, to any fight which might occur in the town, and this one was no exception. He saw the motion and like lightning darted beneath the chair. Once, twice, thrice, his arm rose and fell. Then rushing through the crowd, his right hand above his head grasping a pocket-knife, its blade dripping with blood, he went out into the night, an outcast and a wanderer, a murderer self-baptized in blood. He went out like banished Cain, yet less fortunate than the first murderer inasmuch as there was no curse pronounced against his slayer. His hand was now against every man, and every man's hand against him. He went out forever from the care, the love, and the influence of a fond mother, for he was never to see her face again—she who had so lovingly reared him and whom he had so reverently and tenderly loved. Billy did truly love and revere his mother, and all his after life of crime was marked by deep devotion and respect for good women, born doubtless of his adoration of her.

Alas for Billy! All the good influences were withdrawn from his path. The dove of peace and goodwill to his fellow men could find no resting place in his mind, distorted by fiery passion; and when deadly revenge shook his soul, then he would have plucked the messenger from its perch "though her jesses were his heartstrings". He tripped and fell; he arose with his soul soiled with blood.

The Authentic Life of

CHAPTER II

A Fugitive in Arizona—Picks Up a Partner Named "Alias"—Kills Three Indians for Plunder—A Bunco Horse Race with Indians— Kills a Soldier Blacksmith at Fort Bowie—Flight into Mexico.

AND now we follow our fugitive into Arizona. His deeds of desperate crime in that Territory are familiar to old residents there, but it is impossible to follow them in detail or to give exact dates. It is probable that many of his lawless achievements have escaped both history and tradition. Records of the courts, the Indian Agency, and the military posts, together with reports from officers and citizens, give all the information which can be obtained and cover his most prominent exploits. These reports tally correctly with Billy's disconnected recitals as given to his companions, in after years, to pass away an idle hour.

After the fatal night when Billy first stained his hands with blood and fled his home, he wandered for three days and nights without meeting a human being except one Mexican sheep-herder. He talked Spanish as fluently as any Mexican of them all, and secured from this boy a small stock of provisions, consisting of tortillas and mutton. He was on foot and trying to

8

make his way to the Arizona line; but becoming bewildered, he made a circuit and returned to the vicinity of McKnight's ranch, where he took his initiatory in horse stealing.

The next we hear of Billy shows that some three weeks after his departure from Silver City he had arrived at Fort (then Camp) Bowie, Arizona, with a companion, both mounted on one sore-backed pony, equipped with a pack-saddle and rope bridle, without a quarter of a dollar between them, nor a mouthful of provisions in the commissary. Billy's partner doubtless had a name which was his legal property, but he was so given to changing it that it was impossible to fix on the right one. Billy always called him simply "Alias." With a fellow of Billy's energy and peculiar ideas as to the rights of property, this condition of impoverishment could not continue. After recuperating his enervated physique at the Fort, he and his companion started out on Billy's first unlawful raid. They went on foot, for they had disposed of their pony, and their equipment of weapons consisted of one condemned rifle and one pistol, both borrowed from soldiers.

As is generally known, Fort Bowie is in Pima County, Arizona, and on the Chiracahua Apache Indian Reservation. These Indians were peaceable and quiet at this time, and there was no danger in trusting oneself among them. Billy and his companions fell in with a party of three of these Indians some eight or ten miles south-west of Fort Bowie in the passes of the mountains. A majority of the different tribes of Apaches speak Spanish, and Billy was immediately at home with these. His object was to procure a mount for himself and his companion. He tried arguments, wheedling, promises to pay, and every other plan his prolific brain could suggest; but all in vain. The confidence of these Indians in white man's reliability had been severely shaken in the person of Indian Agent Clum.

Billy gave a vague account of the result of this enterprise, which, though brief and to the point, leaves little to the imagination. Said he: "It was a ground hog case. Here were twelve good ponies, four or five saddles, a good supply of blankets, and five pony loads of pelts. Here were three bloodthirsty savages, reveling in all this luxury, and refusing succor to two free-born, white American citizens, footsore and hungry. The plunder had to change hands—there was no alternative—and as one live Indian could place a hundred United States troops on our trail in two hours, and as a dead Indian would be likely to take some other route, our resolves were taken. In three minutes there were three 'good Injuns' lying around there, careless like, and with ponies and plunder we skipped. There was no fight. It was about the softest thing I ever struck."

The movements of these two youthful brigands for a few days subsequent to the killing of these Indians are lost sight of. It is known that they disposed of the superfluous ponies, equipage, and furs to emigrants from Texas, more than a hundred miles distant from Fort Bowie, and that they returned to the Reservation splendidly mounted and armed and with money in their pockets. They were on the best of terms with government officials and citizens at Fort Bowie, Apache Pass, San Simon, San Carlos, and all the settlements in that vicinity and spent a good deal of their time at Tucson, where Billy's skill as a monte dealer and card player generally kept the two boys in luxuriant style and gave them enviable prestige among the sporting fraternity, which was then a powerful and influential element in Arizona. If anything was known to the authorities of the Indian killing episode, nothing was done about it. No one regretted the loss of those Indians, and no money could be made by prosecuting the offenders.

The quiet life Billy led in the plazas palled on his senses; and, with his partner, he again took the road, or rather the mountain trails. There was always a dash of humor in Billy's adventures, even the most tragical. Meeting a band of eight or ten Indians in the vicinity of San Simon, the two young fellows proposed and instituted a horse race. Billy was riding a very superior animal, but he arranged the race between the inferior horse ridden by his partner and the best horse the Indians had. He even laid a heavy bet on this poor horse of his partner, but took pains to insist that his partner should hold the stakes, consisting of money and revolvers. When the word was given, three instead of two horses shot from the starting point. The interloper was Billy's partner on Billy's horse. He could not restrain the fiery animal, which flew the track, taking the bit in his teeth and never slackening his headlong speed until he reached a deserted cattle ranch many miles away from the improvised race-track.

Billy lost the race, but who was the winner? His partner with all the stakes was "macadamizing" the rocky trails far beyond the ken of the Indians and far beyond successful pursuit. It required all of Billy's Spanish eloquence, all his persuasive powers of speech and gesture, all his sweetest, most appealing expressions of infantile innocence, to convince the untutored and unreasoning savages that he himself was not only the greatest loser of them all, but that he was the

Billy the Kid

victim as well as they of the perfidy of a traitor—to them a heinous crime. Had not he, Billy, taken all the bets and lost them all? While their loss was divided between a half dozen, he had lost his horse, his arms, his money, his friend, and his confidence in humanity, with nothing to show for it but an old plug of a pony that evidently could not win a race against a lame burro. But when did youth and good looks, with well simulated injured innocence, backed by eloquence of tongue and hand-spiced with grief and righteous anger, fail to affect even an Apache? With words of condolence and encouragement from his sympathizing victims, Billy rode sadly away. Two days thereafter, a hundred miles from thence, Billy might have been seen solemnly dividing spoils with his fugitive friend

The last and darkest deed of which Billy was guilty in Arizona was the killing of a soldier blacksmith at Fort Bowie. The date and particulars of this killing are not upon record, and Billy was always reticent in regard to it. There are many conflicting rumors in regard thereto. Billy's defenders justify him on the ground that the victim was a bully, who not only refused to yield up money fairly won from him by Billy in a game of cards, but also precipitated his fate by attempting to inflict physical chastisement on a beardless boy. One thing is sure: this deed exiled Billy

The Authentic Life of

from Arizona, and he is next heard from in the State
of Sonora, Republic of Mexico.

Note A

In one of his talks with J. P. Meadows, Billy the Kid gave
some of the particulars of the killing of the soldier blacksmith.
The Kid, it seems, was dealing monte when the blacksmith,
thoroughly drunken, came in and began to make trouble. The
Kid tried his best to mollify and check the intruder's desire
for a row, but without avail, for the blacksmith finally struck
him a blow that knocked him out of his chair and under the
table. Then, as the Kid expressed it, "I came up a-shooting."

Billy the Kid

CHAPTER III

In Sonora, Billy's knowledge of the Spanish language and his skill in all games of cards practiced by the Mexican people at once established for him a reputation as a first-class gambler and high-toned gentleman. All that is known of his career in Sonora is gathered from his own relation of casual events without detail or dates. He went there alone but soon established a coalition with a young Mexican gambler named Melquiadez Segura which lasted during his stay in the Republic.

During his sojourn in Sonora there was but one fatal encounter of which we have official evidence charged against Billy, and this necessitated his speedy and permanent change of base. This was the killing of Don José Martinez, a monte dealer, over a gaming table. Martinez had for some weeks persistently followed a course of bullying and insult towards Billy, frequently refusing to pay him money fairly won at this game. Billy's entrance to the club room was a signal for Martinez to open his money drawer, take out a six-shooter, lay it on the table beside him, commence a tirade of abuse directed against "Gringos" generally and Billy in particular.

There could be but one termination to this difficulty. Billy settled his affairs in the plaza, then he and Segura saddled their horses, and about nine o'clock at night rode into a *placeta* having two outlets, close by the club room. Leaving Segura with the horses, Billy entered the gambling house. The insult came as was expected. Billy's pistol was in the scabbard; Martinez had his on the table and under his hand. Before he could put his hand on his pistol, the warning came from Billy's lips in steady tones: "José, do you fight as bravely with that pistol as you do with your mouth?" and Billy's hand fell on the butt of his pistol. And here Billy exhibited that lightning rapidity, iron nerve, and marvelous skill with a pistol which gave him such advantage over antagonists and rendered his name a terror even to adepts in pistol practice. Martinez was no coward, but he counted too much on his advantage. The two pistols exploded as one, and Martinez fell back in his seat dead, shot through the eye. Billy slapped his left hand to his right ear, as though he were reaching for a belligerent mosquito. He said afterwards that it felt as though someone had caught three or four hairs and jerked them out.

Before it was fairly realized that Martinez was dead, two horsemen were rushing across the cienega which lies between the plaza and the mountains, and Billy had shaken the dust of Sonora from his feet forever. A party of about twenty Mexicans started immediately in a hot pursuit, which they held steadily for more than ten days. They found the horses ridden from the plaza by Billy and Segura, but horses were plentiful to persons of such persuasive manners as the fugitives. The chase was fruitless and the pursuers returned to Sonora. The family of Martinez offered a large reward for the apprehension and return of Billy to Sonora, and a lesser one for Segura. Several attempts were subsequently made by emissaries of the family to inveigle Billy back there, but the bait was too thin.

The Authentic Life of

CHAPTER IV

In Chihuahua City—A Dead Monte Dealer—*Adios* Chihuahua.

AFTER their flight from Sonora, Billy and Segura made their way to the city of Chihuahua, where their usual good luck at cards deserted them. Billy, it appears, unconsciously made enemies of the gambling fraternity there. Perhaps a little envy of his skill, his powers, and his inimitable style had something to do with it. His difficulties culminated one night. Billy had won a considerable sum of money at a monte table, when the dealer closed his bank and sneeringly told Billy that he did not have money enough in his bank to pay his losses, although he was at that time raking doubloons and double doubloons into a buckskin sack— money enough to pay Billy a dozen times over—and leering at Billy meanwhile.

Billy made no reply, but he and Segura left the house. That monte dealer never reached home with his sack of gold, and his peon who was carrying the sack now lives on the Rio Grande in Mexico in comparatively affluent circumstances. Billy and his partner were seen no more publicly on the streets of Chihuahua

18

Billy the Kid

City, but three other prosperous monte dealers were mysteriously held up at night, as they were returning home from the club rooms, and each was relieved of his wealth. It was afterwards remarked that each of these men had offended either Billy or Segura.

The two adventurers concluded that Chihuahua was not the heaven they were seeking and vanished. Their further movements will be reserved for another chapter, but it may be in place to remark that for some months thereafter the boys settled their little bills along their sinuous route in Spanish gold by drafts on a buckskin sack highly wrought in gold and silver thread and lace in the highest style of Mexican art. As to the monte dealer who so suddenly disappeared, although Billy never disclosed the particulars of the affair, recent advices from Chihuahua give the assurance that the places which knew him there have known him no more since that eventful night. His fellow gamblers speculated at much length upon the disappearance of this dealer who had so openly and defiantly robbed Billy, and they and his family mourn him as dead. Perhaps they do so with cause.

The Authentic Life of

CHAPTER V

Once More a Wanderer—Meets Again with Jesse Evans—Billy's Appearance at Seventeen—A Bloody Fight against a Party of Mescalero Apaches.

AFTER leaving Chihuahua, Billy and Segura went to the Rio Grande, where they parted company but only for a short time. Up to the month of December, 1876, Billy's career was erratic, and it is impossible to follow his adventures consecutively. Many of them are doubtless lost to history. He fell in again with his boon companion, Jesse Evans, and all that is known of Billy's exploits during the ensuing few months is gained from his own and Jesse's disconnected narrations.

This youthful pair made themselves well known in western Texas, northern and eastern Mexico, and along the Rio Grande in New Mexico, by many deeds of daring crime. Young Jesse Evans had already won for himself the reputation of a brave but unscrupulous desperado; and in courage and skill with deadly weapons he and Billy were fairly matched. They were at this time of nearly the same size. Jesse was probably a year or two the oldest, but Billy was slightly the tallest and a little heavier. Billy was seventeen years

Billy the Kid

of age in November, 1876, and was nearly as large as at the time of his death. A light brown beard was beginning to show on his lip and cheeks; his hair was of a dark brown, glossy and luxuriant; his eyes were a deep blue, dotted with spots of a hazel hue, and were very bright, expressive, and intelligent. His face was oval in form, the most noticeable feature being two projecting upper front teeth, which knowing newspaper correspondents who never saw the man or the scenes of his adventures, describe as "fangs, which give to his features an intensely cruel and murderous expression." Nothing could be farther from the truth. That these teeth were prominent features in his countenance is true; that when he engaged in conversation or smiled they were noticeable is likewise true; but they did not give to his always pleasing expression a cruel look or suggest either murder or treachery.

All who ever knew Billy will testify that his polite, cordial, and gentlemanly bearing invited confidence and promised protection—the first of which he never betrayed and the latter of which he was never known to withhold. Those who knew him best will tell you that in his most savage and dangerous moods his face always wore a smile. He ate and laughed, drank and laughed, rode and laughed, talked and laughed, fought and laughed, and killed and laughed. No loud and boisterous guffaw, but a pleasant smile or a soft and musical "ripple of the voice." Those who knew him would always watch his eyes for an exhibition of anger. Had his biographers stated that the expression of his eyes, to one who could read them, was in an angry mood cruel and murderous, they would have shown a more perfect knowledge of the man. One could scarcely believe that those blazing, baleful eyes and that laughing face could be controlled by the same spirit.

Billy was, at this time, about five feet, seven and a half inches high, straight as a dart. He weighed about a hundred and thirty-five pounds and was as light, active, and graceful as a panther. His form was well knit, compact, and wonderfully muscular. It was his delight, when he had a misunderstanding with some one larger and more powerful than himself who feared him on account of his skill with weapons, to unbuckle his belt, drop his arms, and say: "Come on, old fellow. I've got no advantage now. Let's fight it out, knuckles and skull." He usually won his fights; but if he got the worst of it, he bore no malice. There were no bounds to his generosity. Friends, strangers, and even his enemies were welcome to his money, his horse, his clothes, or anything else of which he happened at the time to be possessed. The aged, the

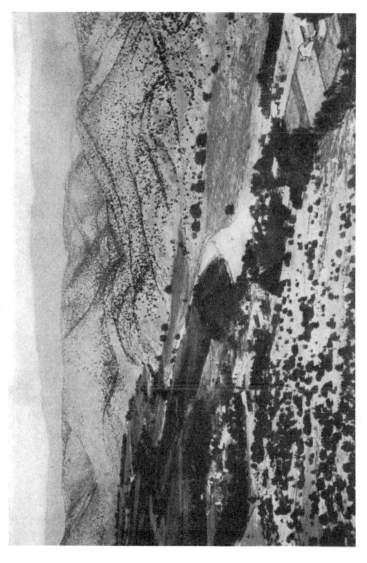

LINCOLN, NEW MEXICO, AND SURROUNDING COUNTRY

This general view, taken from the hills south of the town, shows the section that figured most largely in the Lincoln County troubles, as well as the valley of the Rio Bonito to the west, and the hills and mountains to the northward.

Billy the Kid

poor, the sick, the unfortunate, and the helpless never appealed to Billy in vain for succor.

There is an impression among some people that Billy was excessively gross, profane, and beastly in his habits, conversation, and demeanor. The opposite was the case. It would be strange with Billy's peculiar surroundings if he had not indulged in profanity. He did; but his oaths were expressed in the most elegant phraseology, and, if purity of conversation were the test, hundreds of prominent citizens of New Mexico would have been taken for desperadoes sooner than young Bonney.

Billy was, when circumstances permitted, scrupulously neat and elegant in dress. Some newspaper correspondents have clothed him in fantastic Italian brigand or Mexican guerrilla style, with some hundreds of dollars worth of gold lace, etc., ornamenting his dress; but they did not so apparel him with his consent. His attire was usually of black—a black frock coat, dark pants and vest, a neat boot on his small, shapely foot, and usually a Mexican sombrero—this being his one noticeable peculiarity in dress. He wore this kind of head covering not for show but for convenience. A sombrero is very broad brimmed, protecting the face from the sun, wind, and dust, and is very durable. They are expensive, but Billy never owned one which cost hundreds of dollars. They are worth in Chihuahua from $10 to $50. Some silly fellows with a surplus of money and paucity of brains may have loaded their hats with thousands of dollars worth of metals, gold lace, and thread; but Billy was not one of those.

Billy and Jesse put in the few months they spent together in indulging in numerous lawless raids—sometimes committing depredations in Mexico and fleeing across the Rio Grande into Texas or New Mexico, and *vice versa,* until hundreds of ranchmen in both republics were on the lookout for them. In many conflicts, on either side of the river, they escaped capture and consequent certain death almost by miracle. There was no mountain so high, no precipice so steep, no torrent so fierce, no river so swift, no cave so deep, but these two would essay it in their daring rides for liberty. More than one bold pursuer bit the dust in these encounters, and a price was offered for the bodies of the outlaws dead or alive.

The Mescalero Apache Indians from the Fort Stanton, New Mexico, Reservation used to make frequent raids into Old Mexico and often attack emigrants along the Rio Grande. On one occasion a party from Texas, consisting of three men and their families, on their way to Arizona came across Billy and Jesse in the vicinity of the Rio Mimbres. They took dinner together, and the Texans volunteered much advice to the two supposedly unsophisticated boys, representing to them the danger they braved by travelling unprotected through an Indian country, and finally proposed that they should pursue their journey in company. They gave themselves out to be old and experienced Indian fighters who had in Texas scored their hundreds of dead Comanches, Kickapoos, and Lipans. The boys declined, the slow motion of ox wagons not being to their liking, and after dinner rode on. About the middle of the afternoon, the boys discovered a band of Indians moving along the foothills on the south, in an easterly direction. They speculated on the chances of their new friends, the emigrants, falling in with these Indians, until, from signs of a horse's footprints, they became convinced that an Indian messenger had preceded them from the east; and putting this and that together it became evident to them that the band of Indians they had seen were bent on no other mission than to attack the emigrants.

With one impulse the young knights wheeled their horses and struck across the prairie to the foothills in an attempt to cut the Indian trail. This they succeeded in doing, and found that the party consisted of fourteen warriors, who were directing their course so as to intercept the emigrants or strike them in camp. The weary horses caught the spirit of their brave riders, and over rocks and hills, through canyons and tule brakes, the steady measured thud of their hoofs alone broke the silence.

"Can we make it, Billy?" queried Jesse. "Will our horses hold out?"

"The question is not, will we? but, how soon?" replied Billy. "It's a ground hog case. We've got to get there. Think of those white-headed young ones, Jesse, and whoop up. When my horse's forelegs let up, I've got two of my own."

Just at dusk the two boys rounded a point in the road and came in full view of the emigrants' camp. They were indeed just in the nick of time. At this very moment, the terrible yell of the Apaches broke upon their ears, and the savage band charged the camp from a pass on the south. The gallant horses which had carried the boys so bravely were reeling in their tracks. Throwing themselves out of the saddles, the young heroes grasped their Winchesters; and starting on a run with a yell as blood curdling as any red devil of them all could utter, they threw themselves amongst the yelling fiends. There were astonishment and terror in the cries of the Indians which answered the boys' war cry; and the confusion among the reds increased,

Billy the Kid

as one after another of their number went down under the unerring aim of the two rifles. Jesse had stumbled and fallen into a narrow arroyo overgrown with tall grass and weeds. Raising himself to his knees, he found that his fall was a streak of great good luck. As he afterwards remarked, he could not have made a better entrenchment if he had worked a week. Calling to Billy, he plied his Winchester rapidly. When Billy saw the favorable position Jesse had involuntarily fallen into, he bounded into it; but just as he dropped to his knees a ball from an Indian rifle shattered the stock of his Winchester and inflicted a painful wound on his hand. His gun useless, he fought with his six-shooter—fuming and cursing his luck.

The boys could not see what was going on in the camp, as a wagon intervened; but soon Billy heard the scream of a child as if in death agony and the simultaneous shrieking of a woman. Leaping from his entrenchment he called to Jesse to stay there and cover his attack while he sprang away, pistol in one hand and a small Spanish dagger in the other, directly towards the camp. At this moment the Indians essayed to drive them from their defense. Billy met them more than halfway and fought his way through a half dozen of them. He had emptied his revolver but had no time to load it. Clutching his pistol, he rushed on, and dodging a blow from a burly Indian, he darted under a wagon and discovered lying within reach a prairie ax.

Billy afterwards said he believed his howl of delight at the sight of the ax frightened those Indians so that he and Jesse won the fight. He emerged on the other side of the wagon, where a glance showed him the three men and all the women and children, except one woman and one little girl, ensconced behind the other two wagons and partly protected by a jutting rock. The one woman and the little girl were lying apparently lifeless on the ground. With yell on yell, Billy fell among the reds with his ax. He never missed hearing every crack of Jesse's rifle, and in three minutes there was not a live Indian in sight; while eight "good" ones slept their last sleep. Billy's face, hands and clothing, the wagons, the camp furniture, and the grass were bespattered with blood and brains.

Turning to the camp, the boys discovered that the little girl had possibly received a fracture of the skull in an attempt by an Indian brave to brain her and that the mother had fainted. All three of the men in the party were wounded. One was shot through the abdomen and in the shoulder; it is doubtful whether he survived. The other two were slightly hurt. Billy had

Billy the Kid

the heel of his boot battered, his gun shot to pieces, and received a wound in the hand. Jesse lost his hat; he said he knew when it was shot off his head, but where it went to he couldn't surmise.

The Authentic Life of

CHAPTER VI

Parts Company for Time Being with Jesse—Acquires the By-name, "The Kid"—A Remarkable Ride to the Aid of a Friend—Jail Delivery Single-handed.

AFTER parting with the emigrants whom they had so bravely rescued from the savages, Billy and Jesse changed their course and returned to the Rio Grande. Here they fell in with a party of young fellows well known to Jesse, who urged them to join company with them and go over to the Rio Pecos where they guaranteed they could find remunerative employment. Among this party of cowboys were James McDaniels, William Morton, and Frank Baker, all well known from the Rio Grande to the Rio Pecos. Our two adventurers readily agreed to join fortunes with this party; Jesse did so at once, but Billy delayed a short while. A day or two before they were ready to start he received information that his old partner, Segura, was in the vicinity of Isleta and San Elizario, Texas, and was contemplating going up the Rio Grande to Mesilla and Las Cruces. Billy at once made up his mind to await the coming of his friend, but promised his companions that he would surely meet them in a short time either at Mesilla or in Lincoln County.

Billy the Kid

It was here at Mesilla and by Jim McDaniels that Billy was dubbed the "Kid" on account of his youthful appearance, and under this *nom de guerre* he was known during all his after eventful life. In the future pages of this history he will be designated by this appellation. The Kid's new-found friends accompanied by Jesse left for Lincoln County, and he awaited impatiently the arrival of Segura. He made frequent short trips from Mesilla, and on his return from one of them he led back his gray horse which carried him so gallantly in and out many a tight place during the ensuing two years. It was early in the fall of 1876 that the Kid made his famous trip of eighty-one miles in a little more than six hours, riding the gray the entire distance. The cause and necessity for this journey were as follows:

Segura had been detected in, or suspected of, some lawless act at San Elizario, and had been arrested and locked up in the jail of that town. There were strong prejudices against him there, even by citizens of his own native city, and threats of violence were whispered about. By promises of rich reward, Segura secured the services of an intelligent Mexican boy and started him up the Rio Grande in search of the Kid, in whose cool judgment and boundless courage he placed implicit reliance. He had received a communication from the

Kid a short time before and was about to join him when arrested.

Faithful to his employer, the messenger sought the Kid at Mesilla, Las Cruces, and vicinity, at last finding him on the west side of the Rio Grande about six miles north of Mesilla, and nearly opposite the town of Dona Ana. The distances to San Elizario from this ranch were: to Mesilla, six miles; to Fletch. Jackson's, called the Cottonwoods, twenty-three miles; to El Paso, Texas, twenty-seven miles; and to San Elizario, twenty-five miles; the total being eighty-one miles. The ride doubtless exceeded that distance as the Kid took a circuitous route to avoid observation, but he covered it, whatever the distance, in a little more than six hours, as stated above. He mounted the willing gray at about six o'clock in the evening, leaving the messenger to await his return. He remarked to the boy that he would be on his way back by twelve o'clock that night with Segura. The boy was skeptical, but the Kid patted his horse's neck. "If I am a judge of horse flesh," said he, "this fellow will make the trip," and away he sped.

Avoiding Mesilla, the horseman held down the west bank of the river about eighteen miles to the little plaza of Chamberino, where regardless of fords he rushed into the ever treacherous current of the Rio

Billy the Kid

Grande. More than once the muddy waters almost overwhelmed horse and rider. For thirty minutes or more, the Kid and his trusty gray battled with the angry waves, but skill and strength and pluck prevailed. Horse and rider emerged dripping from the stream full five hundred yards below the spot where they had braved the flood. And now they rushed on, past the Cottonwoods, past that pillar which marks the corner where join Old Mexico, New Mexico and Texas, past Hart's Mills, until the Kid drew rein in front of Ben Dowell's saloon in El Paso,—then Franklin, Texas. It was now a quarter past ten o'clock, and the gray had covered fifty-six miles. The Kid took time to swallow a glass of Peter Den's whiskey and feed his horse a handful of crackers. In ten minutes or in less he was again speeding on his way with twenty-five miles between him and his captive friend. About twelve o'clock—perhaps a few minutes past—one of the Mexicans who was guarding Segura at the lock-up in San Elizario was aroused by a hammering fist and the calling in choice Spanish to open up.

"*Quién es?* (who is that?)," inquired the guard.

"Turn out," replied the Kid. "We have two American prisoners here."

Down rattled the chains and the guard stood in the doorway. The Kid caught him gently by the sleeve

33

and drew him towards the corner of the building. As they walked, the shining barrel of a revolver dazzled the vision of the jailer, and he was notified in a low, steady, and distinct tone of voice that one note of alarm would be the signal for funeral preliminaries. The guard was convinced and quickly yielded up his pistol and the keys. The Kid took the pistol, deliberately drew the cartridges, and threw it on top of the jail. He gave instructions to the jailer and followed him into the hall. The door of the room in which Segura was confined was quickly opened and the occupant cautioned to silence. The Kid stood at the door, cocked revolver in hand, and conversed with Segura in low tones, occasionally addressing a stern command to the frightened guard to hasten, as he bungled with the prisoner's irons.

All this was accomplished in the time it takes to relate it. With the assistance of Segura, the two guards were speedily shackled together, fastened to a post, gagged, the prison doors locked, and the keys thrown up on top of the house, there to rest with the guard's revolver. Declaring himself to be worn out with riding, the Kid mounted Segura on the gray, and then taking a swinging gait, which kept the horse on a lope, they soon left the San Elizario jail and its inmates far behind. Taking a well-known ford, they crossed the

Billy the Kid

Rio Grande and in a little more than an hour were sleeping at the ranch of a Mexican confederate. This friend hid the plucky horse on the bank of the river, mounted a mustang and went in the direction of San Elizario to watch the denouement when the state of affairs should be revealed to the public.

Before daylight the faithful friend stood again before his cabin with the Kid's horse and a fresh, hardy mustang saddled and bridled. Quickly a cup of coffee, a tortilla, and a scrag of dried mutton were swallowed, and again across the prairie sped the fugitives. Two hours later, a party of not less than thirty men armed and mounted rode up to the ranch. The proprietor with many maledictions in pure Spanish launched against "Gringos," "ladrones," related his tale of robbery and insult, how his best horse had been stolen, his wife insulted, and his house ransacked for plunder. He described the villains accurately and put the pursuers on their trail. He saw them depart and returned sadly to his home to mourn in the bosom of his family over the wickedness of the world and to count a handful of coin which the Kid had dropped in making his hasty exit. The pursuers followed the trail surely, but it only led them a wild goose chase across a prairie a few miles, then, making a detour, it made straight for the bank of the Rio Grande again. It was plain to see where the fugitives had entered the stream, but the baffled huntsmen never knew where they emerged. The Kid and his companion reached the ranch where the Mexican boy awaited them about noon the next day. This messenger was rewarded with a handful of uncounted coin and dismissed.

And thus, from one locality after another was the Kid banished by his bloody deeds and violations of law. Yet not utterly banished. It was his delight to drop down occasionally on some of his old haunts in an unexpected hour on his gallant gray, pistol in hand, and to jeer at those officers of the law whose boasts had slain him a hundred times, or to watch their trembling limbs and pallid lips as they blindly rushed to shelter. For all knew and feared Billy the Kid. His look was hardly grim, but through his insinuating smile and fierce blazing eyes enough of determination and devilish fire gleamed to clear the streets though twenty such officers were on duty.

Billy the Kid

CHAPTER VII

A Perilous Journey through the Guadalupe Mountains—Another Encounter with Mescalero Apaches—Almost Miraculous Escape.

WHEN the Kid returned to Mesilla, he found letters from Jesse Evans and his companions urging him to join them on the Rio Pecos near Seven Rivers without delay. They, however, warned him not to attempt the nearer and, under ordinary circumstances, more practicable route by the Guadalupe Mountains, as that country was full of Apache Indians, who always resented encroachments upon their domains. They advised him to follow the mail route by Tularosa and the plaza of Lincoln. The very scent of dangerous adventure and the prospect of an encounter with Indians, who were his mortal aversion, served as a spur to drive the Kid to his destination by the most perilous route. Segura used all his powers of persuasion to divert him from his hazardous undertaking, but in vain. As Segura could not be persuaded to accompany him, they parted again and for the last time.

The Kid now sought a companion bold enough to brave the danger before him, and found one in a young fellow who was known as Tom O'Keefe. He was about the Kid's age, with nerve enough for almost any adventure. These two boys prepared themselves for the trip at Las Cruces. The Kid left his gray in safe hands with the understanding that the pony was to be sent to him upon his order. Though the horse was fleet and long-winded, a common Mexican plug would outdo him in the mountains. So the Kid and O'Keefe procured two hardy mustangs, rode to El Paso, bought a Mexican mule, loaded him with provisions and blankets; and the two seventeen-year-old lads started forth to traverse nearly two hundred miles of Indian country which the oldest and bravest scouts were wont to avoid.

The second night in the mountains they camped at the opening of a deep canyon. At daylight the Kid started out prospecting. He climbed the canyon, and seeing some lofty peaks to the north-west, he labored in their direction with the intention of scaling one of them to determine his bearings. He had told Tom he would return by noon, but he was back in little more than an hour. He announced that he had struck an Indian trail not three hours old and that he was sure that these Indians were making their way to water, not only from the lay of the country but from the fact that they had poured out water on the ground along the trail.

Billy the Kid

"I'll not trouble these redskins to follow me," said the Kid. "I shall just trail them awhile."

"Don't you think," said Tom, "it would be better to take our own trail and follow that awhile?"

"No," replied the Kid. "Don't you see we have got to have water? It's close by. Those breech-clouts are going straight to it. I believe a little flare-up with twenty or thirty of the sneaking curs would make me forget I was thirsty while it lasted, and give water the flavor of wine after the brigazee was over."

"Can't we wait," said Tom, "until they leave the water?"

"Oh," replied the Kid, "we'll not urge any fight with them; but suppose they camp at the springs a week? They'll smell us out ten miles off. I'd rather find them than that they should find us. I am going to have water or blood, perhaps both."

They soon struck the Indians' fresh trail and followed it cautiously for an hour or more, when they suddenly brought up against the bare face of a cliff. The trail was under their feet, leading right up to the rock; but at its base a ragged mass of loose stones were seen to be displaced, which clearly showed the route of the Indians had turned short to the right. By following this, the boys discovered an opening not more than three feet wide, surrounded and overhung with stunted shrubs and clambering vines.

The Kid dismounted and peered through this opening, but could see only a short distance, as his vision was obscured by curves in the pass. They took the back track a short distance; and finding a suitable place of concealment for their animals, they halted. The Kid then took their only canteen and prepared to explore the dreaded pass. He told Tom that if he should return on a run and shouting, the latter should leave the mule and bring out the horse and mount ready to run, "and," said he, "if I bring water don't fail to take the canteen from my hand, drink as you run, and then throw the canteen away."

All Tom's arguments to dissuade the Kid from his purpose were useless. Said he, "I would rather die fighting than to perish from thirst like a rat in a trap." Boldly but cautiously, the Kid entered the dark and gloomy passage. Crouching low, he noiselessly followed its windings some one hundred yards, as he judged, when he suddenly came to an opening about thirty feet wide which stretched away towards the south-west, gradually narrowing until a curve hid its further course from his sight. The passage and opening were walled with rock hundreds of feet high. Grass and weeds were growing luxuriantly in this little amphitheater, and a glance to the left discovered a bubbling mountain spring, gushing forth from a rocky crevice, bright, clear, and sparkling.

Hugging the base of the cliff, creeping on hands and knees, the Kid with canteen in readiness approached the brink of a little basin of rock. The ground about was beaten by horses' hoofs, and water, recently splashed about the margin of the spring, evidenced that the reds had lately quitted the spot. Face and canteen were quickly plunged into the cool stream. The Kid drank long and deep; his canteen was overflowing; and he stealthily moved away. Re-entering the passage, he was congratulating himself on his good fortune, when suddenly a fearful Indian yell and a volley of musketry from almost over his head on the right dispelled his vision of safety. His signal cry rang out in answer; then dashing his canteen in the faces of the Indians, who could only approach singly from the defile, he snatched his six-shooter from its scabbard, wheeled, and, swiftly as any Mescalero of them all, plunged into the gorge he had just quitted, pursued by how many savages he did not know and by yells and showers of lead.

Let us return for a moment to O'Keefe. He heard the Kid's warning shouts, and simultaneously the rattle of fire-arms and the blood-curdling war cry of the Indians. He followed the Kid's instructions so far as to bring the horses out to the trail; then the irresistible impulse of self-preservation overcame him, and he mounted and fled as fast as the sinuous, rugged path would permit. The yells of the bloody Apaches, multiplied by a thousand echoes, seemed to strike upon his ears, not alone from his rear but from the right of him, the left of him, the front of him; and as the outcries resounded from peak to peak, he was persuaded that myriads of dusky devils were in pursuit, coming from every direction.

Spying a cleft in the rocks on his right inaccessible to a horse, he threw himself from the saddle, gave the affrighted mustang a parting stroke which sent him clattering down the steep declivity, then on hands and knees crawled into the chasm. Never casting a look behind, he crept on and up higher and higher, until, as he reached a small level plateau, he thought he had surely attained the very summit of the mountains. The discharge of arms and savage shouts still fell faintly on his ear. Tremblingly he raised himself to his feet. His hands and limbs were scratched, bruised, and bleeding, and his clothing nearly stripped from his body. Faint with loss of blood, exertion, and thirst, he cast his bloodshot eyes over the surrounding crags

Billy the Kid

and peaks. For some moments he could discern no sign of life except here and there a huge bird, startled from his lofty perch by unwonted sounds, lazily circling over the scene of conflict below.

Tom's eyelids were drooping and he was about to yield to an uncontrollable stupor, when his unsteady gaze was caught by a weird, and to him incomprehensible, sight. Away off to the south-east, right on the face of a seemingly perpendicular mountain-side, high up the jagged peak, as though swinging without support in mid-air, he descried a moving object unlike beast or bird, yet rising slowly up and higher up the dizzy cliff. His eye once arrested, he gazed long and steadily until he could clearly discern that it was the figure of a man. Sometimes hidden by the stunted vegetation cropping out from clefts of the rock, and sometimes standing erect in bold relief, he still ascended —slowly, laboriously. Tom could also see masses of rock and earth as they were dislodged by daring feet, and hear them, too, as they thundered down into the abyss below, awaking a thousand echoes from surrounding mountains. It dawned at last upon O'Keefe's bewildered senses that this bold climber could be none other than the Kid and that he had essayed this fearfully perilous ascent as the only means of escape from the Indians. Again Tom's momentarily aroused intellect deserted him, and, utterly exhausted, he sank down upon the rock and slept profoundly.

Let us return to the Kid, whom we left in imminent peril. He had secured a copious draught of water and felt its refreshing effect. He had left his Winchester with Tom, as he was preparing to run and not to fight. Thus he had only his trusty six-shooter and a short dirk with which to make a fight against twenty well-armed savages thirsty for blood. As the Kid darted into the narrow passage which led back to the spring, the Indians were but a few paces behind. But when they reached the opening, their prey was nowhere to be seen. Instinctively they sought his trail and quickly found it. They followed for a few moments silently. The moments were precious ones to the Kid. The trail led them straight up an apparently inaccessible cliff. They involuntarily raised their eyes—and there, as if sailing in open air high above their heads, they descried their quarry. The Kid, however, quickly disappeared behind a friendly ledge, while such a yell of baffled rage went up as only an Apache can utter, and lead rained against the mountain-side, cutting away the scant herbage and flattening against the resisting rock.

In an instant half a dozen young braves were

Billy the Kid

stripped for the pursuit. One, a lithe and sinewy young fellow who appeared to possess the climbing qualities of a panther, quickly reached a point but a few feet beneath where the Kid had disappeared. For one instant an arm and hand projected from the concealing ledge. A flash, a report, and the bold climber poised a moment over the space beneath; then, with arms extended, a death-cry on his lips, he reeled and fell backward, bounding from ledge to ledge, until he lay, a crushed and lifeless mass, at the feet of the band. The Kid next made a feint as if to leave his concealment, thus drawing the fire of the savages, but before their guns were brought to bear on him, he darted back to shelter, again quickly appeared, and amidst yells of hate continued his ascent. Undaunted by the fate of their comrade, the pursuers held steadily on their way. The Kid's body was now stretched forth from his hiding place in full sight with his gaze directed below, and amid a shower of bullets his revolver again belched forth a stream of death-laden fire, and another Apache received a dead-head ticket to the Happy Hunting Grounds. The inert body of this converted savage caught on a projecting ledge and hung over the chasm.

Seeming to scorn concealment, the Kid bent all his energies toward accomplishing the ascent of the precipice, where not even an Apache dared to follow. As

45

he several times paused to breathe, he leaned away out over the yawning gulf beneath, jeering at his foes in Spanish and firing whenever he saw a serape or feather to shoot at. Bullets showered around him as he boldly but laboriously won his way foot by foot. He seemed to bear a charmed life. Not a shot took effect on his person, but he was severely wounded in the face by a fragment of rock rent from the face of the cliff by a bullet.

The actual feats of the veritable Kid strongly resemble those of the fabled Bertram Risingham in his pursuit of the supposed spirit of Mortham, which Sir Walter Scott has so vividly drawn. More than once in clambering up that mountain-side the Kid, like Bertram, trusted his whole weight to his "sinewy hands" and more than once did he dare "an unsupported leap into air." In after days he used to say that the nearest he ever came to having nightmare was in trying to repeat that journey in his dreams. Safely the Kid reached the top of the peak. He felt no fear of pursuit from the Indians, as he knew they had abandoned the perilous route he himself had taken. Furthermore it would require days for them to make a detour so as to intercept him on the south. Yet his situation was forlorn, not to say desperate. Almost utterly exhausted from his exertion, bruised, bleeding,

Billy the Kid

footsore, famishing for food and water, yet what he most craved was sleep and that blessing was accessible. Like O'Keefe, he sank down in a shady nook and wooed "balmy sleep, Nature's sweet restorer."

The Authentic Life of

CHAPTER VIII

WE left the Kid at the end of the last chapter sleeping peacefully on the top of a peak of the Guadalupe Mountains and O'Keefe also asleep on a bench of another peak of the same range. The distance between them in an air line was not so far, but there was more than distance intervening. Canyons, precipices, crags, and brush, to say nothing of a possible band of savages burning with baffled hate and deadly revenge, lay between these two, "so near and yet so far." They both awoke the next morning as the sun appeared in the east and each speculated on the fate of the other. The Kid made a straight break towards the rising sun as soon as he had reached the valley beneath his night's resting place, and reached the cow camps on the Rio Pecos in three days. He procured water at long intervals, but had no food except wild berries during the entire trip. After a few days' rest, having informed himself how his entertainers stood in regard to the two

Billy the Kid

factions in the Lincoln County War, he let them know just who he was, and was immediately armed, mounted, and accompanied to a stronghold of the Murphy-Dolan faction, where he again met Jesse Evans and his comrades, with whom he had parted on the Rio Grande.

The Kid was very anxious to learn the fate of O'Keefe, and induced two or three of the boys to accompany him again to Las Cruces, intending should he hear no tidings of him there to return by the Guadalupe route and try to hunt him up, or, failing in that, to "eat a few Indians," as he expressed it. The Kid never deserted a friend, and it was his friendship for O'Keefe that took him on this trip. But he had another errand at Las Cruces; his favorite gray was there, and he wished to get the horse and bring him back with him to the Pecos section.

Let us go back to O'Keefe in the wild passes of the mountains. Like the Kid, he had slept long and felt refreshed; but, less fortunate than his companion, he had failed to get water the day previous and was suffering intensely from thirst as well as hunger. His first impulse was to place the greatest possible distance between himself and the scene of horror which he had recently witnessed. But his sufferings for lack of water were becoming acute; he felt a sort of delirium and the impulse to return to the spring and procure water was irresistible. Yet he lingered in concealment, listening in terror and suffering untold agony until night fell, when, with the aid of the little light supplied by the moon, he was able to find both the spring and the canteen. Hastily slaking his thirst and filling the canteen, he returned to the spot where he had left the Kid's horse and pack-mule. He found the dead body of the horse, pierced with balls, not a dozen yards from where he had last seen him; but there was no sign of the mule. So Tom had to undertake the task of journeying on foot back to the settlements. Throughout the night and long into the following day he plodded on. Like the Kid, he found a few green berries with which he "fed hunger." Near noon he ran into a deserted Indian camp where they had recently stopped to roast mescal. Poking about among the stones and earth around the pits, he found plenty of half-roasted refuse, which furnished him an ample feast and more than he cared to burden himself with for his after use on the journey.

In a few hours the wanderer reached the level prairie at the foot of the mountains on the south. His good luck was still with him, for in the soft earth he espied the footprints of his own horse which he had deserted. Night was coming on; but, weary as he was, he followed the trail until darkness hid it from view. Just as he was about to seek a "soft place" on which to pass the night, he saw on his right, about a hundred yards away, a moving object. To be brief, it was his own horse, and he slept that night in his saddle blankets, and in due time made his way safely back to the Rio Grande. The meeting at Las Cruces between the Kid and O'Keefe was a surprise and a satisfaction to both. The Kid's efforts, however, to induce Tom to join him in his Lincoln County enterprise were without avail. Tom had seen enough of that locality and did not hanker after a second interview with the Mescaleros.

The Lincoln County War in which the Kid was now about to take a part had been brewing since the summer of 1876 and commenced in earnest in the spring of 1877. It continued for nearly two years, and the robberies and murders consequent thereon would fill a volume. The majority of these outrages were not committed by the principals or participants in the war proper, but the unsettled state of the country incident to these disturbances attracted thither the lawless element—horse and cattle thieves, footpads, murderers, escaped convicts and outlaws—from all the frontier states and territories. At that time Lincoln and the surrounding counties offered a rich and a comparatively safe field for their nefarious operations.

It is not the intention here to discuss the merits of the embroglio or to censure or uphold either one faction or the other, but merely to detail such events of the war as the hero of these adventures took part in. The principals in this difficulty were on one side John S. Chisum, called the Cattle King of New Mexico, with Alexander A. McSween and John H. Tunstall as important allies. On the other side were the firm of Murphy & Dolan, merchants at Lincoln, the county seat, backed by nearly every small cattle owner in the Pecos Valley. This latter faction was supported by Thomas B. Catron, United States Attorney for the Territory, a resident of Santa Fe, one of the eminent lawyers of the Territory, and a considerable cattle owner in the Pecos region.

John S. Chisum's herds ranged up and down the Rio Pecos, from Fort Sumner to way below the line of Texas, a distance of over 200 miles, and were estimated to number from 40,000 to 80,000 head of full-blooded, graded, and Texas cattle. Alexander McSween was a successful lawyer at Lincoln who was often retained by Chisum and who had other pecuniary interests with the Pecos Valley Cattle King. John H. Tunstall was an Englishman who only came to this country in 1876. He had ample means at his command and formed a partnership with McSween at

VIEWS IN LINCOLN, NEW MEXICO

Upper, the stretch of the single street of Lincoln between the Tunstall-McSween store and the Murphy-Dolan-Riley store. The house to the right of the Tunstall-McSween store is a later building. *Lower left,* Patron's store and saloon; *lower right,* Montana store.

Billy the Kid

Lincoln, the firm erecting two fine buildings and establishing a mercantile house and "The Lincoln County Bank" there. Tunstall was a liberal, public-spirited citizen, and seemed destined to become a valuable acquisition to the reliable business men of this section. He had also, in partnership with McSween, invested considerably in cattle.

This bloody war originated about as follows: The smaller cattle owners in the Pecos Valley charged Chisum with monopolizing as a right all this vast range of grazing country. They claimed also that his great avalanche of hoofs and horns engulfed and swept away their smaller herds without hope of recovery or compensation; in other words, that the big serpent of this modern Moses swallowed up the lesser serpents of these magicians. They maintained that each round up of Chisum's vast herd carried with it hundreds of head of cattle belonging to others. On Chisum's part, he claimed that these smaller proprietors had combined together in a system of reprisals to round up and drive away from the range, selling them at various military posts and elsewhere throughout the country, cattle which were his property and which bore his mark and brand. Collisions were frequent from time to time between herders in the employ of the opposing factions, and, as above stated, in the winter and spring of 1877 the war commenced in earnest. Robbery, murder, and bloody encounters soon ceased to excite either horror or wonder. Under this state of affairs it was not so requisite that the employees of these stockmen should be experienced *vaqueros* as that they should possess courage and the will to fight the battles of their employers even to the death.

The reckless daring, the unerring marksmanship, and unrivalled horsemanship of the Kid rendered his services a priceless acquisition to the ranks of the faction that could secure him. As related already, he was first enlisted by McDaniels, Morton, and Baker, who were adherents to the Murphy-Dolan cause. Throughout the summer and a portion of the fall of 1877, the Kid faithfully followed the fortunes of the party to which he had attached himself. His time was spent on the cattle ranges of the Pecos Valley and on the trail, with occasional visits to the plazas, where with his companions he indulged without restraint in such dissipations as the limited facilities of the little *tendejones* afforded. His encounters with those of the opposite party were frequent; and his dauntless courage and skill rapidly won for him name and fame, which either admiration or fear or both, forced his friends, as well as his enemies, to respect. No especially noteworthy event occurred during the Kid's adherence to the Murphy-Dolan faction, and he declared afterwards to his friends that all the uses of his life during that time were "flat, stale, and unprofitable."

The Kid was certainly dissatisfied with his connection. Whether conscientious scruples oppressed his mind, or whether policy dictated his resolve, he finally determined to desert his employers and the cause in which he was engaged and in which he had done yeoman's service. He met John H. Tunstall, a leading factor of the opposition. Whether the Kid sought this interview, or Tunstall sought him, or whether it came about by chance, is not known. At all events, our hero expressed to Tunstall his regret for the course he had pursued against him, and offered him his future services. Tunstall immediately put him under wages and sent him to the Rio Feliz, where he had a herd of cattle.

The Kid rode back to camp and boldly announced to his associates that he was about to forsake them and that when they should meet again they would be in bitter enmity. Dark and lowering glances gleamed out from beneath contracted brows at this statement, and the Kid half-dreaded and half-expected a bloody ending to the colloquy. Angry expostulation, eager argument, and impassioned entreaty all failed to shake his purpose. Perhaps the presence and intervention of his old and tried friend, Jesse Evans, stayed the threatened explosion.

"Boys," argued Jesse, "we have slept, drank, feasted, starved, and fought cheek by jowl with the Kid. He has trusted himself alone among us, coming like a man to notify us of his intention. He didn't sneak off like a cur and leave us to find out when we heard the crack of his Winchester that he was fighting against us. Let him go. Our time will come; we shall meet him again, perhaps in fair fight,"—then he added under his breath, "and he'll make some of you brave fellows squeak."

Silently and sullenly the rest of the party acquiesced except Frank Baker, who insinuated in a surly tone that now was the time for the fight to come off. "Yes, you damn cowardly dog!" replied the Kid, "right now, when you are nine to one. But don't take me to be fast asleep because I look sleepy. Come on, Baker, if you are stinking for a fight; you never killed a man that you did not shoot in the back. Come and fight a man that's looking at you." The Kid's eyes flashed lightning as he glared on the cowering Baker who answered not a word. With this banter on his lips, the Kid slowly wheeled his horse and rode leisurely away,

casting one long regretful glance at Jesse, from whom
he was loath to part.

Note A

Viewed through the longer perspective of nearly fifty years,
the Lincoln County War seems to have originated in a different
manner from the way Garrett puts it. When he wrote, the
view expressed by him had wide currency, and even today, in the
reminiscences of old timers and in the later histories of New
Mexico, there is a strong tendency to say that the Lincoln
County War was primarily a war between the large cattlemen,
like John S. Chisum, and the smaller cattlemen, of whom
there were an increasing number in Lincoln County. It is
true that, beginning possibly with the year 1876, acute situa-
tions had frequently arisen in quarrels over range rights and in
affrays growing out of cattle stealing, but these did not develop
into large enough proportions to be called a feud, and it is doubtful whether they would have done so even in the course of
time. These conditions, however, unquestionably did much
toward preparing the ground for the Lincoln County War
proper.

The incident that precipitated the feud was the cowardly
and brutal murder of the young Englishman, John H. Tunstall, which Garrett mentions in the next chapter. The motive back of this affair was business rivalry and personal ill-
feeling on the part of members of the firm in Lincoln, known
at that time as J. J. Dolan & Co., although many still used
the earlier designation L. G. Murphy & Co., or merely the
names of the most conspicuous of the partners, Murphy and
Dolan, toward the newer and flourishing business organization
of J. H. Tunstall & Co., which included besides Tunstall,
Alexander A. McSween, a successful lawyer of Lincoln who
was beginning to branch out into several business ventures.
For five or six years, Murphy and Dolan had dominated all
that part of the county commercially and politically and they
were not disposed to brook competition from the new firm,

which in the few months of its career through straightforward and honest methods had made great inroads on the business of the older firm.

This hostility first focussed itself upon the Englishman Tunstall inasmuch as he was supposed to be the main source of the capital which was being used by J. H. Tunstall & Co. He was "bumped off" in the way described in the next chapter, and immediately thereafter the whole county became aligned into two factions known commonly as the Murphy and Dolan (although Murphy himself was so besotted with drink that he was not a very active participant) and the McSween. The encounters between the partisans of these two groups during the next six or eight months make up what is commonly understood as the Lincoln County War.

At the start, McSween was not so conspicuous a factor as Tunstall, but gradually he became more and more an element in the situation. Murphy and Dolan were quick to seize a chance to discredit him in connection with what was commonly called "the Fritz money." Colonel Emil Fritz, one of the partners in the original L. G. Murphy & Co., had died while on a visit to Germany in 1874. The settlement of his estate dragged along for several years, and in 1876 McSween was employed by the administrators to collect an insurance policy for $10,000. To accomplish this he had to make a trip to New York City and to employ the assistance of lawyers there. The policy was eventually paid in full, and the New York attorneys informed McSween that they had credited his account with $7,148.94, that being the proceeds of the policy after the deduction of their fees. Against this sum McSween claimed $4,095.15 for his fee and the expenses of his trip to New York. This claim seems to have been allowed by the Probate Judge as a just one, but for some reason McSween did not make settlement for the balance with the Fritz estate. This situation was capitalized by Murphy and Dolan in their capacity of general advisors to the Fritz heirs living at Lincoln, Charles Fritz and Mrs. Scholand, and used as a means to secure both the arrest of McSween on the charge of embezzlement and the wholesale attachment of all his property in Lincoln, including that which he owned jointly with Tunstall, and even of some property that was clearly Tunstall's in his own right.

These steps against McSween preceded by a few days the killing of Tunstall and were contributory to it. The whole situation at Lincoln had become highly inflamed and was likely on the slightest provocation to break out into lawlessness. John Chisum, sixty miles away in the Pecos Valley, who had been friendly and intimate with both Tunstall and McSween in personal and business ways, naturally stood with his friends, and was generally credited with furnishing various kinds of aid and comfort to this side. It seems, however, that he was not really a personal participant in the Lincoln County War and that none of his employees took any part in it with his sanction, although some of them were participants on their own responsibility. As a matter of fact, Chisum was out of Lincoln County during the months when the feud was most active. He had undergone arrest and lodgment in jail at Las Vegas in the early part of January, 1878, because he was unwilling to meet the demands of a suit which was being prosecuted by Thomas B. Catron, then the United States District Attorney, growing out of alleged partnership in a packing house firm that had been established at Little Rock, Arkansas. Chisum remained in jail, it seems, until the latter part of March; then he returned to Lincoln County, but after a few months left for an extended absence.

Garrett is one of the few writers on the Lincoln County War who has had the frankness and the courage to mention Catron's name in connection with it. His is the figure which looms up behind the Murphy and Dolan faction. As the president of the powerful First National Bank at Santa Fe, he furnished the money needed by Murphy and Dolan in their business, of course taking mortgages which at the close of the War gave him possession of their store and its stock of goods. Catron was also a cattle raiser, and in some sense a dominating figure in that industry in the western part of the county. Besides all this he was a powerful member of the clique of politicians and business men called in those days the "Santa Fe Ring," which largely controlled the Territory of New Mexico.

59

CHAPTER IX

The Kid's Apparent Reformation While in Tunstall's Employ—
Tunstall's Cowardly Murder—The Kid Swears Vengeance—
Partially Carries Out His Vow in Killing Morton and Baker.

AFTER pledging allegiance to Tunstall the Kid plodded on for some months in the monotonous groove fashioned for the cowboy. In his bearing one would never detect the daredevilism which had heretofore characterized him. He frequently came into contact with his employer and entertained for him a strong friendship and deep respect which were fully reciprocated by Tunstall. The Kid was also ever a welcome guest at the residence of McSween. Both Tunstall and McSween were staunch friends of the Kid, and he was faithful to them to the last. His life passed on uneventfully. Deeds of violence and bloodshed were of frequent occurrence on the Pecos and in other portions of the country, but all was quiet on the Rio Feliz where Tunstall's ranch was. The Kid seemed to have lost his taste for blood. He was passive, industrious, and seemingly content. But it was the lull before the storm.

In the month of February, 1878, William S. Mor-

Billy the Kid

ton (said to have had authority as deputy sheriff) with a posse of men composed of cowboys from the Rio Pecos started out to attach some horses which Tunstall and McSween claimed. Tunstall was on the ground with some of his employees. On the approach of Morton and his party, Tunstall's men all deserted him—ran away in fact. Morton afterwards claimed that Tunstall fired on him and his posse; at all events, Morton and his party fired on Tunstall, killing both him and his horse. One Tom Hill, who was afterwards killed while robbing a sheep outfit, rode up as Tunstall was lying on his face gasping, and placing his rifle to the back of his head, fired, and scattered Tunstall's brains over the ground.

This murder occurred on the 18th of February, 1878. Before night the Kid was apprised of his friend's death. His rage was fearful. Breathing vengeance, he quitted his herd, mounted his horse, and from that day to the hour of his death his track was blazed with rapine and blood. The Kid rode to Lincoln and sought McSween. Here he learned that R. M. Brewer, sworn in as special constable and armed with a warrant, was about to start with a posse to arrest the murderers of Tunstall. The Kid joined this party, and they proceeded to the Rio Pecos.

On the 6th of March, Brewer and his posse

jumped up a party of five men below the crossing on the Rio Peñasco and about six miles from the Rio Pecos. They fled and the officer's party pursued. The pursued broke into two groups, and the Kid, recognizing Morton and Baker in two of the fugitives who composed one of the groups, took their trail and was followed by his companions. For fully five miles the desperate flight and pursuit was prolonged. The Kid's Winchester belched fire continually, and his followers were not idle; but distance and the motion of running horses disconcerted their aim, and the fugitives were unharmed. Suddenly however their mounts stumbled, reeled, and fell almost at the same instant. Perhaps the horses were wounded; no one paused to see. A friendly sink-hole in the prairie close at hand served the fleeing pair as a breastworks from which they could have stood off twice the force following them. And yet the pursuers had the best of it, as the pursued had but two alternatives—to surrender or to starve.

After considerable parley, Morton said that, if the posse would pledge their word of honor to conduct himself and his companion, Baker, to Lincoln in safety, they would surrender. The Kid strongly opposed giving this pledge. He believed that two of the murderers of Tunstall were in his power, and he thirsted for their blood. But he was overruled, the pledge was given, the prisoners were disarmed and taken to Chisum's ranch. The Kid rode in the advance, and as he mounted was heard to mutter, "My time will come."

On the 9th of March, 1878, Brewer with his posse and prisoners left Chisum's for Lincoln. The party numbered thirteen men—the two prisoners, special constable R. M. Brewer, J. G. Scurlock, Charlie Bowdre, the Kid, Henry Brown, Frank McNab, Fred Wayt, Sam Smith, Jim French, John Middleton, and Wm. McCloskey. They stopped at Roswell, five miles from Chisum's, to give Morton an opportunity to mail a letter at the postoffice there. This letter he registered to a cousin, Hon. H. H. Marshall, Richmond, Va. A copy of this letter is in the hands of the author, as well as a letter subsequently addressed to the postmaster by Marshall. Morton was descended from the best blood of Virginia, and left many relatives and friends to mourn his loss. Morton, together with all the rest of the party, was well known to the postmaster, M. A. Upson, and Morton requested him, should any important event transpire, to write to his cousin and inform him of the facts connected therewith. Upson asked him if he apprehended danger to himself on the trip. He replied that he did not, as the posse had pledged themselves to deliver him and Baker to the authorities at Lincoln. But he added that, in case this pledge was violated, he wished his people to be informed. McCloskey of the Brewer posse was standing by, and rejoined, speaking to Morton, "Billy, if harm comes to you two they will have to kill me first."

The Kid had nothing to say; he appeared distrait and sullen, evidently "digesting the venom of his spleen." After a short stay, the cortège went on its way. This was the last ever seen of these two unfortunates alive, except by the special constable and his posse. It was about ten o'clock in the morning when they left the postoffice. About four o'clock in the evening, Martin Chaves of Picacho arrived at Roswell from above and reported that the trail of the party showed they had left the direct road to Lincoln and turned off in the direction of Agua Negra (Black Water). This was an unfrequented route to the base of Sierra Capitan, and the information at once settled all doubts in the minds of the hearers as to the fate of Morton and Baker.

On the 11th, Frank McNab, one of the posse, returned to Roswell and entered the postoffice. Upson said to him, "Hello, McNab, I thought you were in Lincoln by this time. Any news?"

Billy the Kid

"Yes," replied he, "Morton killed McCloskey, one of our men, and made a break to escape; so we had to kill them."

"Where did Morton get weapons?" inquired Upson.

"He snatched McCloskey's pistol out of its scabbard, killed him with it, and ran, firing back as he went. We had to kill them or some of us would have been hurt," explained McNab.

This tale was too attenuated. Listeners did not believe it. The truth of the matter as related by the Kid, in which he was supported by several of his comrades, was as follows: It had been resolved by two or three of the guards to murder Morton and Baker before they reached Lincoln. It has been stated by newspaper correspondents that the Kid killed McCloskey. This report is false. The Kid was not one of the conspirators nor did he kill McCloskey. He had cursed Brewer in no measured terms for giving a pledge of safety to the prisoners, but he said that as it had been given it must be kept. He further expressed his intention to kill them both and said the time would come for him to fulfill this threat, but that he would not murder unarmed men.

McCloskey and Middleton constantly rode close upon the prisoners as if to protect them; the others brought up the rear, except the Kid and Bowdre, who were considerably in advance. About twenty or thirty miles from Roswell, near the Black Water Holes, McNab and Brown rode up to McCloskey and Middleton. McNab placed his rifle to McCloskey's head and said, "You are the son of a b—— that's got to die before harm can come to these fellows, are you?" and fired as he spoke. McCloskey rolled from his horse a corpse. The terrified, unarmed prisoners fled as fast as their sorry horses could carry them, pursued by the whole party and a shower of harmless lead. At the sound of the shot, the Kid wheeled his horse. All was confusion. He couldn't take in the situation. He heard fire-arms, and it flashed across his mind that perhaps the prisoners had in some unaccountable manner got possession of weapons. He saw his mortal enemies attempting to escape, and as he sank his spurs into his horse's sides he shouted to them to halt, but they held on their course with bullets whistling around them. A few bounds of the infuriated gray carried him to the front of the pursuers. Twice only his revolver spoke, and a life sped at each report. Thus died McCloskey, and thus perished Morton and Baker. The Kid dismounted, turned Morton's face up to the sky and gazed down on his old companion long and in silence. He asked no questions and the party rode on to Lincoln, except McNab, who returned to Chisum's ranch. They left the bodies where they fell. They were buried by some Mexican sheep-herders.

NOTE A

As indicated in the note to the preceding chapter, the incident that precipitated the Lincoln County War was the cold-blooded murder of John H. Tunstall. With an Englishman's love of honesty and fair play, and with something of the Englishman's outspokenness, Tunstall had in an open letter, published in the Mesilla *Independent,* charged that Brady, the sheriff of the county, had deposited county tax money with Murphy and Dolan and that they had used this money in settlement of some of their obligations. Tunstall had also announced that he proposed to go before the next grand jury and make further exposures regarding Brady as well as regarding Murphy and Dolan.

Tunstall had also incurred the enmity of a notorious band of cattle thieves and cutthroats, known as the "Seven Rivers Warriors," which embraced Jesse Evans, sometimes called "Captain" because of his position of leadership, his brother, George Davis, Tom Hill, and Frank Baker. While Tunstall was away on a trip to St. Louis in the summer or fall of 1877, these men had stolen horses from his Rio Feliz ranch, and Tunstall had forced Brady to arrest them and confine them in the jail at Lincoln. They easily made their escape through the connivance of the sheriff, for they were likewise henchmen of Murphy and Dolan, and had been going about the county making threats against Tunstall's life in retaliation for their arrest.

On February 9th, Brady, acting under the attachment order issued against McSween, took charge of all McSween's personal and real property in Lincoln, and even went so far as to attach the store of J. H. Tunstall & Co. and its entire stock. Not satisfied that he had secured in this way enough property to cover the sum involved in the Fritz money affair, Brady sent on February 12th a small posse in charge of Billy Matthews down to Tunstall's Rio Feliz ranch to attach the cattle there. Dick Brewer, Tunstall's foreman, refused to deliver the cattle and denied that there were any there that belonged to McSween. Brewer went so far, however, as to promise Matthews that the latter might return a few days later, accompanied by only one man, and have a chance to investigate and see if any of the cattle belonged to McSween.

Tunstall, who was at the time in Lincoln trying to straighten out matters regarding his store and have it released from the sheriff's hands, learned that Matthews, with the support of the members of the J. J. Dolan & Co. firm, was raising a large posse in the Pecos Valley with the intention of returning to his ranch and seizing the cattle. Tunstall sensed danger in this move, for he had heard rumors that a certain member of the rival firm had said it was "no use for Tunstall and McSween to try to escape this time." So on February 16th Tunstall started from Lincoln for his ranch and reached it on the 17th. He ordered his men to let the deputy sheriff's posse take the cattle, his intention being to save bloodshed and have the ownership of the cattle settled in the courts. He decided however to drive to Lincoln some eight or ten horses that he considered especially valuable.

Early on the morning of the 18th, Tunstall started back to Lincoln, taking the horses and accompanied by four of his employees, Dick Brewer, R. A. Widenmann, John Middleton, and William H. Bonney. Shortly after his departure, Billy Matthews arrived at the ranch with his large posse. Finding Tunstall gone, he, with the advice of Dolan, decided to divide the posse into two groups, one to remain at the ranch and take charge of the cattle, while the other was to follow Tunstall, ostensibly to take the horses. In this smaller group were Tunstall's implacable enemies, the Jesse Evans quartette. They had not been formally summoned to the posse by Matthews, but there was no decided protest to their presence and to their going along with the smaller posse on the pretext that they wanted to recover from among Tunstall's horses some that belonged to them. The smaller posse was placed under the command of William S. Morton, foreman of the Murphy cattle camp on the Pecos.

About five o'clock in the afternoon the Morton posse overtook the Tunstall party. Brewer, Widenmann, and Tunstall were driving the horses, while Middleton and Bonney were riding along some six hundred yards in the rear. Just a few minutes before the Morton posse appeared, Brewer and Middleton had ridden about three hundred yards to one side after a flock of wild turkeys. When the posse topped the hill behind Tunstall's party, their hostile attitude was apparent enough to Tunstall's companions, and seeing the futility of resistance, they all rode for safety among the trees and boulders on a neighboring hillside. As they dashed in that direction, Middleton, according to his own version of the matter, rode close to Tunstall and shouted, "For God's sake, follow me!" Tunstall apparently did not understand what was expected of him, for Middleton heard him ask perplexedly, "What, John? What, John?"

What happened in the next few minutes is not known with certainty beyond the fact that Tunstall then lay dead on the ground with a wound in the left breast and another in the back of his skull. It is generally supposed that Morton, as the leader of the posse, called to Tunstall to stop, saying that he wanted to see him and would not hurt him. Thereupon Tunstall dismounted and walked toward Morton. Knowing the custom of such occasions, Tunstall extended his revolver to Morton. Almost immediately one of the Seven Rivers Warriors, some say Jesse Evans, others, Tom Hill, took aim at Tunstall and shot him through the breast. As he fell forward, Morton fired, using Tunstall's own revolver, the bullet entering the back of Tunstall's head and coming out in his forehead. Morton then walked up to Tunstall's horse and shot the animal with Tunstall's pistol. Tunstall's body and that of the horse were then laid side by side, and the posse rode back to Tunstall's ranch to report to Billy Matthews that Tunstall had resisted Morton and had met his death in the resulting affray.

At the session of the grand jury in the following April indictments for the murder of Tunstall were returned against Jesse Evans, George Davis, Frank Rivers, and Miguel Segorio, while indictments were returned against Dolan and Matthews as accessories to the murder. All of these had their trials postponed and were released under bond. When court next convened in the spring of 1879, the four in the group under indictment for murder could not be found and their bond was declared forfeited. Dolan and Matthews had their cases continued under a change of venue to Socorro County.

NOTE B

The capture of Morton and Baker took place late of an afternoon, and the Brewer posse went with the two prisoners for the night to one of the Chisum cattle camps in that vicinity. The next day they journeyed up to the Chisum ranch at Spring River, where they spent the second night, and possibly the next day or two. There is unimpeachable testimony showing that all in the Brewer party, even including the Kid, were disposed to treat the two prisoners in a fair and kindly way.

But Brewer and his group were getting more and more into a quandary as to the course to pursue. If they carried out their original intention and returned to Lincoln with Morton and Baker, what then? Knowing the attitude of the sheriff, Brady, they realized that if they turned the prisoners over to him, it would not be long until they were freed under some pretext. And once more at liberty, what guarantee was there that Morton and Baker and their associates might not seek revenge on Brewer, the Kid, and the others who had participated in the capture? Such questions as these were the topics in the discussions among the Brewer party at Chisum's ranch.

Furthermore, disquieting rumors were coming down from Lincoln. A vague general report was to the effect that Murphy and Dolan had collected a body of men, the number being put as high as seventy, and were determined to complete the removal of their rivals by killing both McSween and his friend, Chisum. A more definite rumor had it that Murphy and Dolan, having heard of the capture of Morton and Baker, were sending a force down to Chisum's to effect a release. Brewer is said to have received a definite message to this effect after he had left Chisum's for Lincoln, and it was this report that caused him to go in the direction of Black Water. The change in route might therefore be interpreted as not being made to find a remote spot where they might kill the prisoners, but rather to find a refuge for a few days until they could see what developments might take place at Lincoln, and at the same time be close enough to the town to have, in case of need, the aid of the full force of McSween adherents.

In the light of these circumstances, the killing of Morton and Baker does not seem premeditated and deliberate. The quarrel with McCloskey, which precipitated the shooting, was a natural result of the impression that Brewer's men had that McCloskey was a spy and trouble-maker. He had not been present when Morton and Baker had been taken prisoners, but had joined the posse while it was staying at Chisum's ranch. There had been discussion as to whether McCloskey should be allowed to stay and go up to Lincoln with them. McCloskey was one of the employees on Tunstall's ranch, but he had not been selected to go to Lincoln with him on the 18th of February. When the Morton posse had been chosen to pursue Tunstall, McCloskey had gone along with them until he had been compelled to drop behind because of his horse's giving out. He had not therefore been with the posse when it met and killed Tunstall. But his actions had created suspicion as to which side he was really on.

Public sentiment seems to have condoned the killing of Morton and Baker. The Murphy faction, of course, secured justice of the peace warrants against most of the members of the Brewer posse, but when the grand jury met in April, 1878, it took no official notice of the killing of Morton and Baker and returned no indictments.

NOTE C

The letter Morton wrote to his kinsmen in Virginia happens to be preserved and is given below as an interesting document in these happenings. In it, he clings to the story that he and his associates had concocted about the killing of Tunstall.

South Spring River, N. M.
March 8, 1878.

H. H. Marshall,
Richmond, Va.,

Dear Sir:

Some time since I was called upon to assist in serving a writ of attachment on some property wherein resistance had been made against the law.

The parties had started off with some horses which should be attached, and I as deputy sheriff with a posse of twelve men was sent in pursuit of same. We overtook them, and while attempting to serve the writ our party was fired on by one J. H. Tunstall, the balance of the party having ran off. The fire was returned and Tunstall was killed. This happened on the 18th of February.

The 6th of March I was arrested by a constable's party, accused of the murder of Tunstall. Nearly all of the sheriff's party fired at him, and it is impossible for any one to say who killed him. When the party which came to arrest me, and one man who was with me, first saw us about one hundred yards distant, we started in another direction when they (eleven in number) fired nearly one hundred shots at us. We ran about five miles, when both of our horses fell and we made a stand. When they came up they told us if we would give up, they would not harm us.

After talking awhile, we gave up our arms and were made prisoners. There was one man in the party who wanted to kill me after I had surrendered, and was restrained with the greatest difficulty by others of the party. The constable himself said he was sorry we gave up as he had not wished to take us alive. We arrived here last night enroute to Lincoln. I have heard that we were not to be taken alive to that place. I am not at all afraid of their killing me, but if they should do so, I wish that the matter should be investigated and the parties dealt with according to law. If you do

Billy the Kid

not hear from me in four days after receipt of this, I would like you to make inquiries about the affair.

The names of the parties who have me arrested are: R. M. Brewer, J. G. Skurlock, Chas. Bowdre, Wm. Bonney, Henry Brown, Frank McNab, "Wayt," Sam Smith, Jim French (and two others named McClosky and Middleton who are friends). There are two parties in arms and violence is expected. The military are at the scene of disorder and trying to keep peace. I will arrive at Lincoln the night of the 10th and will write you immediately if I get through safe. Have been in the employ of Jas. J. Dolan & Co. of Lincoln for eighteen months since the 9th of March '77 and have been getting $60.00 per month. Have about six hundred dollars due me from them and some horses, etc. at their cattle camps.

I hope if it becomes necessary that you will look into this affair, if anything should happen, I refer you to T. B. Catron, U. S. Attorney of Santa Fe, N. M. and Col. Rynerson, District Attorney, La Mesilla, N. M. They both know all about the affair as the writ of attachment was issued by Judge Warren Bristol, La Mesilla, N. M. and everything was legal. If I am taken safely to Lincoln, I will have no trouble, but will let you know.

If it should be as I suspect, please communicate with my brother, Quin Morton, Lewisburg, W. Va. Hoping that you will attend to this affair if it becomes necessary and excuse me for troubling you if it does not,

I remain

Yours respectfully

W. S. Morton

Lincoln,
Lincoln Co. N. M.

The Authentic Life of

CHAPTER X

The Kid Bears a Part in the Buckshot Roberts Encounter—Becomes Leader of the Band upon the Death of Brewer—A Clash in Lincoln with Billy Matthews—Killing of Sheriff Brady and His Deputy, Hindman.

RETURNING to Lincoln, the Kid attached himself to the fortunes of McSween, who was every day becoming more deeply involved in the events of the war. McSween was a peaceably disposed man, but the murder of his partner aroused all the belligerent passion within him. The Kid still adhered to Brewer's posse, as his hunger for vengeance was by no means satiated and Brewer was still on the trail of Tunstall's murderers.

One of the actors in that tragedy was an ex-soldier named Andrew L. Roberts who was generally called Buckshot Roberts from the fact that he carried in his body many bullets, relics of previous fights. The Kid heard that he could be found in the vicinity of the Mescalero Apache Indian Agency at South Fork, some forty miles south of Lincoln. Roberts was a splendid shot, an experienced horseman, and as brave as skillful. Brewer and party were soon on their way to at-

74

Billy the Kid

tempt his arrest. The Kid knew that Roberts would never be taken alive by Brewer's posse when the fate of Morton and Baker at their hands was so fresh in his memory. To the Kid this was a strong incentive, for it was lives he wanted, not prisoners. As the party approached the building from the east, Roberts came galloping up from the west. The Kid espied him, and bringing his Winchester on his thigh, he spurred directly towards Roberts as Brewer demanded a surrender. Roberts' only reply was to the Kid's movements. Quick as lightning his Winchester was at his shoulder and a bullet sang past the Kid's ear. The Kid was as quick as his foe and his aim more accurate; the bullet from the rifle went crashing through Roberts' body, inflicting a mortal wound. Although hurt to the death, this brave fellow was not conquered but lived to wreak deadly vengeance on the hunters.

Amid a shower of bullets, he dismounted and took refuge in an outhouse from whence while his brave life lasted he dealt death from his rifle. He barricaded the door of his weak citadel with a mattress and some bedclothing which he found therein, and from this defense he fought his last fight. His bullets whistled about the places of concealment where lurked his foes. Wherever a head, a leg, or an arm protruded, it was a target for his rifle. Charlie Bowdre was severely wounded in the side, a belt of cartridges about his body saving his life. At this point in the fight Dick Brewer met his death. Doctor Blazer's sawmill was directly across the street from Roberts' hiding place. In front of the mill were lying numerous huge saw-logs. Unseen by Roberts, Brewer had crept behind these to get a shot at him. But no sooner did Brewer raise his head to take an observation than the quick eye of Roberts detected him. Only one of Brewer's eyes was exposed, yet it was enough. A bullet from Roberts' Winchester found entrance there, and Brewer rolled over dead behind the saw-log. Roberts' time was short, but to his last gasp his eye was strained to catch sight of another target for his aim, and he died with his trusty rifle in his grasp.

To the Kid the killing of Roberts was neither cause for exultation nor grief. He had further bloody work to do. He swore he would not rest nor stay his murderous hand so long as one of Tunstall's slayers lived. With Brewer dead, the command of the squad by common consent was conferred upon the Kid. He had little use for the position, however, except as it threw around his deeds the protection of the law which he held in such disdain. All that he wanted to accomplish his purpose were two or three "free riders" who without fear or compunction would take their lives in their hands and follow where he might lead.

On their return to Lincoln, the posse was disbanded, but most of those composing it joined fortunes with the Kid as their accepted leader. With his emissaries riding over the country in every direction, he bided his time and opportunity. Most of the while he was in Lincoln and frequently met adherents of the other faction, which meetings were ever the signal for an affray. Jacob B. Matthews, well known throughout the Territory as Billy Matthews, held the Kid in mortal aversion. He had not been with the posse that killed Tunstall, but he had denounced in no measured terms the killers of Morton, Baker, and Roberts. He was an intimate friend of popular Jimmy Dolan of the firm of Murphy & Dolan and a strong supporter of their cause. Billy was as brave as any red-handed killer of them all. On the 28th of March he was in Lincoln Plaza, and, as chance would have it, unarmed. On the street he happened to come suddenly face to face with the Kid, who immediately cut down on him with his Winchester. Billy darted into a doorway, which the Kid shot into slivers about his head. Matthews had his revenge, though, as will hereafter appear.

At this time William Brady was sheriff of Lincoln

County. Major Brady was an excellent citizen and a brave and honest man. He was a good officer too, and endeavored to do his duty with impartiality. The objections made against Sheriff Brady were that he was strongly prejudiced in favor of the Murphy-Dolan faction—those gentlemen being his warm personal friends—and that he was lax in the discharge of his duty through fear by giving offense to one party or the other. Sheriff Brady held warrants for the Kid and his associates, charging them with the murders of Morton, Baker, and Roberts. The Kid and his accomplices had evaded arrest by dodging Brady when they were in the plaza and by standing guard in the field. They resolved to end this necessity for vigilance and plotted a crime which would disgrace the record of an Apache. The Kid had become a monomaniac on the subject of revenge for the death of Tunstall. There could be no deed so dark and damning but he would achieve it if it would enable him to remove obstacles from the path leading to the accomplishment of his revenge. Brady with his warrants was one of these obstacles, and his fate was therefore sealed.

On the 1st of April, 1878, Sheriff Brady, accompanied by George Hindman and Billy Matthews, started from Murphy & Dolan's store in Lincoln to go to the courthouse, and there announce that no court would be held at the stated April term. In those days of anarchy a man was seldom seen on the streets of Lincoln without a gun on his shoulder. The sheriff and his companions each bore a rifle. The Tunstall & McSween store stood about half way between the two above-named points. In the rear of the Tunstall & McSween building was a corral, the east end of which projected beyond the house and commanded a view of the street along which the sheriff had to pass. The Kid and his accomplices had cut grooves in the top of the adobe wall in which to rest their guns. As the sheriff came in sight, a volley of bullets were poured upon him and his two companions from the corral; Brady and Hindman fell, while Matthews took shelter behind one of the old houses on the south side of the street. Brady was killed outright, being riddled with bullets. Hindman was mortally wounded, but lived a few moments.

Ike Stockton, who was for so long a terror in Rio Arriba County, this Territory, and in southern Colorado, and who was recently killed at Durango, kept a saloon in Lincoln Plaza at the time this killing occurred and was supposed to be a secret ally of the Kid and his gang. Witnessing the killing, he approached the fallen men. Hindman called faintly for water. The Rio Bonito was close at hand, and Stockton brought water to the wounded man in his hat. As he raised Hindman's head, he discovered Matthews in the latter's place of concealment. At this moment the Kid and his fellows leaped from the corral wall and approached the two bodies with the intention of taking possession of the arms of Brady and Hindman.

Ike knew that as soon as they came in the range of Matthews' vision the latter would fire on them, and he was equally sure that if he were to divulge to the Kid Matthews' whereabouts, he would himself become a target. So he fenced a little, trying to persuade the Kid that he had better not disturb the arms, or at least to defer the taking of them for a while. The Kid, however, was determined, and as he stooped and raised Brady's gun from the ground, a bullet from Matthews' rifle dashed it from his hand and plowed a furrow in his side, inflicting a painful though not dangerous wound. For once the Kid was nonplussed. To approach Matthews' place of concealment was to court death, and it was equally dangerous to persevere in his attempt to possess himself of Brady's and Hindman's arms. Discretion prevailed, and the Kid and his party retired to the house of McSween. This murder was a most dastardly crime on the part of the Kid, and

Billy the Kid

lost him many friends who had heretofore excused and screened him.

NOTE A

In the case of the Roberts encounter, Garrett's chronology, which is usually remarkably correct, happens to be wrong. The fight took place on April 4th, a few days after the killing of Brady, the sheriff. Brewer and his companions had left Lincoln after the assassination of Brady, for the simple reason that it was safer to be elsewhere. Some accounts state that Brewer and his followers were determined to wipe out the entire judicial machinery of the county because they believed it was favorable to Murphy and Dolan. So, after killing the sheriff, they had gone west to intercept and kill the judge, Warren Bristol, and the district attorney, Rynerson, who were journeying to Lincoln from Mesilla for the approaching session of court.

There is diversity of opinion as to the cause of the attack on Roberts, even the Kid, according to J. P. Meadows, afterwards confessing that it was not clear to him why the fight started. Roberts had, however, been in the posse that went to Tunstall's ranch, although he had not been with the smaller posse that followed and killed Tunstall. The temper of the Kid and the others with Brewer being what it was towards any one at all implicated in the Tunstall murder, it is easy to see a ground for trouble with Roberts. But whatever the reason for the encounter, the result was one of the most desperate fights waged by one man against overwhelming odds that western history shows. Even the Kid in later years, when reminiscing over the affair, said to J. P. Meadows, "Yes, sir, he licked our crowd to a finish," and expressed his admiration for the courage and tenacity shown by Roberts.

A conflict of opinion exists as to which of the Brewer posse was responsible for the killing of Roberts. The Kid claimed that he fired the shot that gave Roberts his mortal wound, but Roberts himself in a dying statement asserted that Bowdre had fired the shot that struck him.

81

The Authentic Life of

The murder of Brady, the sheriff of Lincoln County, in such a cold-blooded manner startled the whole state of New Mexico as nothing that had heretofore happened in Lincoln County had done. There was apparently no motive for it except that Brady had harassed the Kid and his followers until they were ready to take desperate measures to be rid of him. Garrett's encomium of Brady must be qualified by the statement that Brady, although inclined to be conscientious in the discharge of his duties, was decidedly under the domination of Murphy and Dolan, and their wishes were almost law to him.

McSween strongly condemned the murder and upbraided the Kid for his part in it. At the time, McSween was at Chisum's ranch, and came into Lincoln later in the day on which Brady was killed. Many have wondered that the Brady murder did not bring about a break between McSween and those implicated in it, especially the Kid. But McSween was interested in bringing to justice those who had killed Tunstall and in securing for Tunstall's family in England an indemnity. The Kid was one of his star witnesses, and for that reason McSween did not think he could dissociate himself from him.

When court convened about a week after the killing of Brady, the grand jury gave this affair first place on its calendar, and brought in indictments therefor against John Middleton, Henry Brown, and the Kid. Middleton and Brown left the state shortly afterwards and nothing further was done toward bringing them to trial. The Kid voluntarily surrendered to Sheriff Kimbrell in March, 1879, and was brought to Lincoln for trial. But the case was continued for some reason, and the Kid escaped from custody. He was not apprehended again until December, 1881, when he surrendered to Garrett at Stinking Spring. His trial and conviction for the murder of Brady took place in April, 1881, at Mesilla, as related in a subsequent chapter of this book.

Billy the Kid

NOTE C

Garrett's remark that the sheriff was on his way to the court-house to announce that no term of court was to be held in April is a loose statement of the circumstances. The April term of court was held a few days later, and there seems never to have been any intention on the part of Judge Bristol to omit that session. But through a clerical error the jury venire had been made returnable on the first Monday of April whereas court usually convened on the second Monday. Brady was probably on his way to the courthouse to inform any of the jury who had arrived at Lincoln that such a mistake had been made.

NOTE D

The Kid's implacable animosity toward Billy Matthews is easily explainable by the part Matthews had taken in the Tunstall murder. He had been prominent in that affair, although he had not been of the party in at the death. Brady placed him in charge of the first posse that went to Tunstall's Rio Feliz ranch and continued him in charge of the second and larger posse that reached the ranch on the 18th of February.

The Authentic Life of

CHAPTER XI

Bowdre Captured by Jesse Evans' Party—The Kid to the Rescue—
Dramatic but Bloodless Encounter between the Kid and Evans.

THE Kid and his desperate gang were now out-lawed in Lincoln, yet they haunted the plaza by stealth and always found a sure and safe place of conceal-ment at McSween's. The laws were not administered, and they even dared to enter the plaza in broad day, defying their enemies and entertained by their friends. For some space Lincoln had no sheriff. Few were bold enough to attempt the duties of the office. At length, George W. Peppin consented to receive a temporary appointment. He appointed, in his turn, a score of deputies; and during his tenure of office, robbery, murder, arson, and every crime in the calendar united and held high carnival in Lincoln. The Kid was not idle. Wherever a bold heart, cool judgment, skillful hand, or reckless spirit was required in the interests of his faction, the Kid was in the van.

San Patricio, a small Mexican plaza on the Rio Ruidoso, some seven miles from Lincoln by a trail across the mountains, was a favorite resort for the Kid and his band. Most of the Mexicans there were friendly to him and kept him well informed as to any movement which might jeopardize his liberty. José Miguel Sedillo, a faithful ally of the Kid, brought him information one day in June about daylight that Jesse Evans with a party from below was prowling about, probably with the intention of stealing a bunch of horses belonging to Chisum and McSween which were in charge of the Kid and his party.

Without waiting for breakfast, the Kid started with five men, all who were with him at that time. They were Charlie Bowdre, Henry Brown, J. G. Scurlock, John Middleton, and Tom O'Folliard. This latter was a young Texan, bold and unscrupulous, who followed the fortunes of the Kid from the day they first met literally to the death. At this time he had only been with the gang a few days. Taking Brown with him, the Kid ascended a ridge on the west of the Ruidoso and followed it up toward the Brewer ranch where he had left the horses. He sent Bowdre in charge of the other three of the party with instructions to follow the river up on the east bank.

After riding some three miles, the Kid heard firing in the direction where Bowdre and his men should be. The shots were scattering as though a skirmish were in progress. He dismounted and sent Brown on ahead to circle a hill on the left, while he himself led his gray down the steep declivity toward the river and rode in the direction of the shooting. With much difficulty, he reached the foot of the mountain, crossed the river, and was laboriously climbing the steep ascent on the east, when the clatter of a single horse's feet arrested his attention; and in a moment through a gap of the hills he descried Brown riding furiously towards the north, and at the same instant a fusillade of fire-arms saluted his ears.

He mounted, and then came a most wonderful ride of less than a mile. It was not remarkable for speed but the wonder is how he made it at all. Through crevices of rock it would seem a coyote could scarcely creep into, over ragged precipices, through brush, cactus and zacaton, he made his devious, headlong way, until, leaving the spur of hills he had with such difficulty traversed, another similar elevation lay in front of him, while between the two was a gorge some half mile across, and at the foot of the opposite hill was the scene of the conflict. Jesse, with a band of eight men, had attacked Bowdre's party. They were fighting and skirmishing among the rocks and undergrowth at the foothills and were so mixed and confused and hidden that the Kid could scarce distinguish friends from foes. He spied Bowdre, however, in the hands of the enemy, among whom he recognized Jesse, and with one of his well-known war cries to cheer his friends, he dashed madly through the gorge.

Bowdre's account of previous events showed how Evans and his men attacked him about two miles from the hills. Having an inferior force, he made a run for the foothills and took a stand there among the rocks and brush. Several shots were fired during the chase. Evans made a detour of the hills to avoid the range of Bowdre's guns, and the skirmish commenced. Bowdre became separated from his men. He saw Brown as he rode to the rescue, and sought ambush on the east of the hill. Evans also saw Brown, and sent a shower of lead after him, which was the volley that reached the ears of the Kid and brought him to the scene. Thinking to join Brown who had not recognized him, Bowdre broke from cover on a run, but fell into the hands of Jesse and four of his men.

He was powerless against numbers and his only hope was to stand Evans off until assistance arrived. How he prayed for the appearance of the Kid as he shot anxious glances around! No shot was fired; Evans and party covered him with their revolvers, and Jesse's merry blue eyes danced with boyish glee, albeit a little devil lurked about the corners, as he bantered his prisoner:

"Where's your pard, Charlie? I expected to meet him this morning. I am hungry and thought I would slay and roast the Kid for breakfast. We all want to hear him bleat."

Bowdre choked back the retort which rose to his lips. He was dismounted and his gun taken from the scabbard where he had replaced it when surprised; but his captors made no motion to relieve him of his revolver. Bowdre stood with his hand resting on his horse's haunch. Three of Evans' men were dismounted, and two of their horses stood heads and tails, each bridle rein thrown over the other's saddle horn.

At this moment it was that the Kid's well-known yell rang out like the cry of a panther. The Evans crowd seemed paralyzed, and Bowdre remarked, "There comes your breakfast, Jesse." All gazed wonderingly at the sight of a gray horse, saddled and bridled, dashing across the valley, with no semblance of a rider save a leg thrown across the saddle and a head and arm protruding from beneath the horse's neck, while at the end of this arm the barrel of a pistol glistened in the sunlight. Quicker than it can be told, the gray dashed among the amazed gazers.

Billy the Kid

The Kid's voice rang out, "Mount, Charlie, mount!"
He straightened himself in the saddle and drew rein,
but before he could check his headlong speed, the
powerful gray had breasted the two horses which were
hitched together and thrown them heavily. One
mounted man lost his seat and fell beneath his horse.
Triumph in his eye, Bowdre had seized his gun un-
noticed and had mounted, ranging himself beside the
Kid.

This meeting was a sight not soon to be forgotten
by those who witnessed it. These two young beardless
desperadoes, neither of them yet twenty-one years of
age, boyish in appearance but experienced in crime,
of nearly equal size, had each earned a reputation for
desperate daring by desperate deeds which had made
their names a terror wherever they were known. They
had slept together on the prairies, by camp-fires, in
Mexican pueblos, and on the mountain-tops. They
had fought the bloody Mescaleros and Chiricahuas side
by side; they had shared their last dollar and their last
chunk of dried deer meat, and had been partners in
many other reckless and less creditable adventures
since their earliest boyhood. No one would have
thought from their smiling faces that these two were
mortal foes. Their attitudes were seemingly careless
and unconstrained, as they sat their chafing horses,

each with a revolver at full cock in his right hand resting on his thigh. Though their eyes twinkled with seeming mirth, they were on the alert. Not for an instant did each take his eye from the other's face. As their restless horses champed the bit, advanced, retreated, or wheeled, that steady gaze was never averted. It seemed their horses understood the situation and were eager for the strife. Thus for a moment they gazed. There was a little sternness in the Kid's eye, despite its inevitable smile. Jesse at length laughingly broke the silence.

"Well, Billy, this is a hell of a way to introduce yourself to a private picnic party. What do you want, anyhow?"

"How are you, Jesse?" answered the Kid. "It's a long time since we met. Come over to Miguel Sedillo's and take breakfast with me. I've been wanting to have a talk with you for a long time, but I am powerful hungry."

"I, too, have been wanting to see you," responded Jesse, "but not exactly in this shape. I understood you were hunting the men who killed that Englishman, and I wanted to say to you that neither I nor any of my men were there. You know, if I had been, I would not deny it to you or any other man."

"I know you wasn't there, Jesse," replied the Kid.

Billy the Kid

"If you had been, the ball would have been opened here without words."

"Well, then," asked Jesse, "what do you jump us up in this style for? Why, you'd scare a fellow half to death that didn't know you as well as I do."

"Oh, ask your prisoner here—Charlie," said the Kid. "He'll tell you all about it. You won't go to breakfast with me, then? Well, I'm gone, but one word, Jesse, before I go. There's a party from Seven Rivers lurking about here; they are badly stuck after a bunch of horses I have been in charge of. The horses are right over the hills there at Brewer's old ranch. If you meet that crowd, please say to them that they are welcome to the horses; but I shall be there when they receive them and shall insist that they take Old Gray and some other horses along, as well as me and a few choice friends. Come, put up your pistol, Jesse, and rest your hand."

With these words, the Kid slowly raised his pistol hand from his thigh, and Jesse as deliberately raised his. The dancing eyes of Jesse were fixed on the Kid, and the darker, pleasant, yet a little sterner, eyes of the Kid held Jesse's intently. Simultaneously the muzzles of their pistols were lowered, neither for an instant pointing in the direction of the other; then with the spontaneous movement of trained soldiers they dropped their weapons into the scabbard. As they raised their hands and rested them on the horns of their saddles, seven breasts heaved a sigh of relief.

"I have some more men scattered about here," remarked Jesse.

"And so have I," replied the Kid. "Now, Jesse, you ride down the arroyo," pointing east as he said this, "and I will ride to the top of the hills," pointing west. "I'll get my men together in a moment and I suppose you can herd yours. No treachery, Jesse. If I hear a shot, I shall know which side it comes from. Old Gray does not care in which direction he carries me, and he can run."

With these words, the Kid reined in his horse toward Rio Ruidoso and without turning his head rode leisurely away. Bowdre sat a moment and watched Evans whose eyes followed the Kid. Jesse, at last, wheeled his horse, and ejaculating, "By God, he's a cool one," called to his followers and dashed down the arroyo. Bowdre rejoined the Kid, and in twenty minutes the party of six were reunited and were trotting merrily with sharpened appetites to breakfast. Thus ended this bloodless encounter. It was incomprehensible to their followers that these two leaders could meet without bloodshed; but the memory of old times

must have come over them and curbed their bold
spirit. Had one act of violence been proffered by
either of the leaders, they would certainly have fought
it out to the bloody, fatal end.

NOTE A

The interval during which there was no sheriff lasted only a
few days. McSween saw to it that the county commissioners
appointed John N. Copeland, and when court convened on
the 10th of April, he was formally sworn in. The selection
of Copeland, however, was a thorn in the flesh of the Murphy-
Dolan faction because he was regarded as a sympathizer of
the McSween crowd. So they used their influence with Governor Axtell and finally secured the removal of Copeland.
The Governor's proclamation to this effect was dated May
28th, and alleged as ground for the action that Copeland had
failed to make proper bond as collector of taxes. George
W. Peppin was then designated by the Governor as sheriff in
Copeland's place. This act on the part of Governor Axtell
became, as much as any one thing, the ground of his removal
from the governorship by President Hayes and the appointment
in his stead of General Lew Wallace.

NOTE B

This interview between the Kid and his whilom companion
Jesse Evans should not be the less dramatic for the editor's
being under the necessity of labelling a part of the final conversation as probably apocryphal. Jesse Evans, together with
other members of the Seven Rivers Warriors, were present at
the killing of Tunstall, and Jesse Evans was one of those suspected of having fired the first shot that killed Tunstall,
although there were many indications that Tom Hill was
responsible for it.

The Authentic Life of

CHAPTER XII

The Desperate Three Days' Fight at Lincoln—Burning of the Mc-Sween Residence—The Kid Makes a Sortie—Fights His Way from the Burning Building and Escapes—Death of McSween.

DURING all this time Sheriff Peppin was not idle but could do little toward restoring peace in the distracted county. In selecting his deputies, he had chosen some brave and reliable business men upon whom he could depend. Among these was Marion Turner of the firm of Turner & Jones, merchants at Roswell. Turner had been for years, off and on, in the employ of Chisum, who had reposed great confidence in him and had valued his services highly. Turner had been a staunch adherent of Chisum at the beginning of the trouble and had continued such until May, 1878, when he seceded for what he probably deemed sufficient cause and became one of his old employer's bitterest enemies. Turner had control of the sheriff's operations in the valley of the Rio Pecos and soon raised a posse of between thirty and forty men, composed principally of cattle owners and cowboys, few of whom knew the taste of fear.

Turner's headquarters were at Roswell, where the

posse was encamped. Early in July, the Kid with fourteen men visited Chisum's ranch, five miles from Roswell. Turner and his force went there with the intention of ousting the Kid from his stronghold. But he found this impossible, as the houses on the place were built with a view to defense against Indians and a band of fourteen determined men could hold it against an army, barring artillery. Consequently Turner relinquished his attempt on the ranch but kept spies constantly on the alert. A few days later he received information that the Kid had left Chisum's and had started up the Pecos towards Fort Sumner. Turner had several warrants for the Kid, and now he swore either to arrest him or to kill him or to die in the attempt. So with his full force he took the trail; but, after riding some twenty miles, he pronounced this movement of the Kid's to be a blind, and turning west, he left the trail and took a short cut straight out to Lincoln.

The result proved his sound judgment, for the Kid and his band were in Lincoln, safely barricaded in the elegant and spacious residence of McSween and prepared to stand a siege and defend their position to the last. Sheriff Peppin with a few recruits joined Turner at the "Big House," as the Murphy & Dolan store was called; but Turner was the ruling spirit of the enterprise. For three days spasmodic firing was kept up from both sides, but no harm was done. On the morning of July 19, 1878, Turner expressed his intention of going to the house of McSween and demanding the surrender of the Kid and others against whom he had warrants. This plan his companions denounced as foolhardy, and they predicted that he would be shot down before he got within speaking distance. Nothing daunted, Turner persisted in his design and called for volunteers to accompany him. His partner, John A. Jones, than whom a braver man never lived in New Mexico, at once offered to accompany him and his example was followed by eight or ten others.

As Turner's party advanced, they saw the dangerous portholes in the side of the building, but to their surprise they were allowed to walk up to the walls and ensconce themselves between these openings without being hailed or receiving a hint that their presence was suspected by those within. The explanation of this circumstance was that the besieged were at that time holding a council of war in a room in the rear where the whole garrison was assembled. The result of their discussion was that the spirit of the Kid, who had sworn that he would never be taken alive, swayed the more timid, and it was resolved to drive off the assailants or to die at their posts. McSween appeared to be inert, expressing no opinion or desire. As they returned to their posts, they were astonished to find the front yard occupied by their foes. The Kid hailed the intruders, whereat Turner promptly notified him that he held warrants for the arrest of William H. Bonney and others of his companions, among them Alexander A. McSween. The Kid replied, "We, too, have warrants for you and all your gang which we will serve on you hot from the muzzles of our guns." In short, the Kid and all his confederates refused to make terms. Turner himself then retired to safety, but not so, however, his attendants. They did not propose to relinquish the position they had gained, and in a few minutes the fight commenced in earnest.

At this juncture, Lieut. Col. Nathan A. M. Dudley of the 9th Cavalry arrived from Fort Stanton nine miles distant with a company of infantry and another of artillery. Planting his cannon in a depression of the road between the Murphy & Dolan store on the west and the McSween house on the east, he announced that he would turn his guns loose on the first of the two belligerent parties that fired over the heads of his command. Nevertheless the fight went on, and the big guns remained silent.

Turner was confident and said he would have the Kid out of there if he had to burn the house down over his head. The Kid on his part was sanguine, saying he could stand the besiegers off, and acting as gayly as if he were at a wedding. Both men knew that the struggle would be a bloody one and neither anticipated an easy victory. Turner's men took possession of all the surrounding buildings, from which they kept up a desultory firing which was returned by those in the McSween mansion. Doors, windows, and other outside woodwork were slivered by flying bullets, and earth flew from the adobe walls. This fusillade from the besiegers was aimed at covering the operations of those of their allies who had remained in the yard and who were laboring to fire the building by working kindlings under door and window sills and wherever woodwork was exposed. Some of the Kid's party had climbed to the roof, and from behind the parapets harassed the foe with their firing. To drive these from their position Turner sent a dozen men to the hills which overlook the plaza on the south, and their heavy long-range guns soon dislodged the Kid's sharpshooters. A magnificent piano in one of the front rooms was hit several times by these marksmen on the hillsides, and at each impact sent forth discordant sounds. This circumstance elicited from

SCENES IN AND ABOUT LINCOLN, HAVING CONNECTION
WITH THE LINCOLN COUNTY WAR

Upper, San Patricio, a Mexican plaza a few miles across the mountains, which was a frequent place of refuge for the Kid. *Middle,* remains of the torreon at Lincoln, a round stone fortification originally built for protection from Indians, which became of strategic importance during the Lincoln County feud. *Lower,* approximate location of the graves of Tunstall, McSween, and Morris, whose deaths came from this feud. These graves are behind the old adobe wall of the corral to the Tunstall-McSween store.

Billy the Kid

a Lamy, New Mexico, correspondent of the New York *Sun* the following:

> "During the fight Mrs. McSween encouraged her wild garrison by playing inspiring airs on her piano and singing rousing battle songs, until the besieging party, getting the range of the piano from the sound, shot it to pieces with their heavy rifles."

The truth is that Mrs. McSween and three lady friends left the house before the fight commenced. It is also true that she requested permission to return for some purpose, and when this had been granted, the firing ceased until she had gone inside and fulfilled her mission. When she had left the house, the firing was resumed.

About noon the flames burst forth from the front doors and windows, and the fate of the building was sealed. All efforts by the inmates to extinguish the blaze were fruitless, and the assailing party shouted their joy. Soon the whole front of the house was deserted by its defenders, and Jack Long, procuring a little coal oil—less than a gallon in fact—made his way into a room that was not yet on fire, and carefully saturating the furniture with the oil, set fire to it and made his escape. This small quantity of coal oil set the Lamy correspondent off again:

> "On the third day of the skirmish Turner had the house fired by throwing buckets full of blazing coal oil into it and over it."

Doesn't it seem that buckets full of blazing coal oil would be hard to handle? An adobe building burns very slowly, and this was a large one containing eleven rooms; but the flames relentlessly and surely drove the inmates back into the east wing of the house. Every few minutes the besiegers would call on them to surrender, but their only reply would be curses and defiance.

When night set in, the defenders of the house had but one tenable room left, a kitchen at the back of the house, and it would furnish shelter for but a short time. The question of surrender was discussed and vetoed by the Kid with scorn. Bloody, half-naked, begrimed with smoke and dust, his reckless spirit was untamed. Fiercely he threw himself in the doorway, the only means of escape, and swore that he would brain and drag back into the burning building the first man that made a motion to pass that door. "Hold on," he said, "until the fire breaks through upon us. Then all as one man, we'll break through this door, take to the undergrowth on the Rio Bonito, and from there to the hills. We'll have an even chance with them in the bottom." This *ipse dixit* settled it. The Rio Bonito was not more than fifty yards from the back of the house and the measure suggested seemed altogether within the range of possibility.

Billy the Kid

Shortly afterwards, however, one affrighted Mexican, disregarding the Kid's threat, precipitated the bloody finale. He called out to stop shooting and they would surrender. A blow from the Kid's revolver, and the presumptuous fellow lay bruised and senseless on the floor; but the Kid did not have time to execute all his threat. Just as soon as the Mexican's voice was heard by those on the outside, the firing ceased. Robert W. Beckwith, a cattle owner from Seven Rivers, accompanied by John Jones, passed round the corner of the main building in full view of the kitchen doorway. No sooner did Beckwith appear than a shot from inside the house inflicted a wound on his hand. Seeing the Kid and McSween in the door, he shouted, "McSween! McSween!" and opened fire on them. The Kid shot but once, and Beckwith fell dead, the ball entering near the eye.

The Kid called, "Come on," to his companions; and leaping over Beckwith's prostrate body, he fought his way, pistol in hand, through a score of enemies. Step by step he fought his way to the brink of the river, into which he plunged and soon was among the weeds and brush on the other side. He was followed by all his band who had life and strength to flee, and several who did so left a bloody trail in their wake. McSween, less fortunate than the Kid, fell dead in the yard, pierced with nine bullets. Tom O'Folliard, the new recruit, was the last one to leave the yard, and he showed his pluck by stopping to pick up a friend, Harvey Morris. Discovering that he was dead, O'Folliard dropped the body, and through a shower of lead made his escape unharmed.

This all happened about 10 o'clock at night. The fight for the present was ended, the building was in ashes, several mangled corpses lay about, and several on both sides nursed desperate wounds. Turner's party had lost but one man killed besides Beckwith. The Kid's party had suffered five casualties, McSween, Morris, and three Mexicans. Turner's party numbered about forty men and the Kid's nineteen, aside from McSween.

NOTE A

No adequate account of the three days' fight at Lincoln has been written. Garrett's résumé is meager, but it suggests the determination and courage shown by both sides. The fight won admiration from Col. Dudley, experienced Civil War soldier that he was. In his official report he writes of his expectation that the feud will persist and comments on the Lincoln fight as follows:

"Men who have the reckless courage to attack a building in bright mid-day, its walls forming a perfect protection against any modern musketry to its inmates, pierced as this castle of McSween's was with scores of loopholes for rifles on every side and angle, to say nothing of the flat roof protected by a perfect wall of defense, and for hours hugging

Billy the Kid

the walls exposed to the fire not only from the loopholes but from the roof and adjacent buildings held by McSween's men, charging this position across a space perfectly exposed to the fire of McSween's men for a distance of nearly 300 yards, are not of a character to be easily induced to abandon a course they believe is only half completed.

"A similar remark can be made of the party holding this structure who held the same fortification for five days, the last nine hours gradually retreating from one room to another as the heat compelled them to do what no amount of leaden missiles from the rifles of the attacking party could do and for one hour finally, all huddled in one room nearly surrounded by the flames, some, as it is claimed, preferring to be burnt rather than surrender to the sheriff's posse. More desperate action than was exhibited on this unfortunate day by both sides is rarely witnessed."

The Authentic Life of

CHAPTER XIII

The Killing of Bernstein at the Indian Agency—Fort Sumner Be-
comes Headquarters for the Kid's Gang—The Kid Calls Long's
Bluff—Horse and Cattle Stealing Expeditions—Threats against
Chisum—Arrest at Lincoln and Easy Escape from Jail—The Kid
and Jesse Evans Meet Again—Murder of Chapman by Dolan
Partisans.

AFTER the deplorable events detailed in the last
chapter, the Kid gathered together such of his gang
as were fit for duty and took to the mountains south of
Lincoln. From thence they made frequent raids, stealing horses and mules in the vicinity of Dowlin's Mill,
the Indian Agency, Tularosa, and the Pecos Valley,
and occasionally varying the monotony by taking a
few ponies from the Mescaleros. They became very
bold in their operations, even approaching the Agency
without fear.

On the 5th of August, 1878, they rode up in full
sight of the Agency, and were coolly appropriating
some horses, when the bookkeeper, named Bernstein,
mounted a horse and said he would go and stop them.
He was warned of his danger by persons who knew
the Kid and his gang, but unheeding he rode boldly

up and commanded them to desist. The only reply
was from the Kid's Winchester, and poor Bernstein
answered for his temerity with his life. This gentleman was a Jew, well known in the Territory. He had
been in the employ of Speigelberg Brothers and of
Murphy & Dolan previous to his connection with the
Agency and was an excellent business man and accomplished gentleman.

Sheriff Peppin together with his posse had retired
from active service after the bloody 19th of July, and
law was a dead letter in the county. Immediately after
the killing of Bernstein, the Kid, accompanied by
O'Folliard, Fred Wayt, Middleton, and Brown, went
to Fort Sumner, San Miguel County, on the Rio Pecos,
eighty-one miles north of Roswell. Here they established a rendezvous to which they clung to the last
chapter of this history. Bowdre and Scurlock, who
had married Mexican wives who were devoted to
them and followed their fortunes faithfully, remained
in Lincoln County for some time. But, in the absence of their leader, they were careful to avoid pub-
licity. In the meantime the Kid and his friends applied themselves industriously to the pursuit of pleas-
ure in and around Fort Sumner. They worshipped
religiously at the shrines of Bacchus and Venus, but
only for a brief space. They had arrived at Sumner

on the 18th of August, but by the 1st of September, this party of five had started back for Lincoln in order to assist Bowdre and Scurlock to remove their families to Sumner. This business was accomplished without any adventure of moment.

On the 10th of September, the Kid with three of his party again left Sumner for Lincoln County, this time bent on plunder. Charlie Fritz, who lived on a ranch eight miles east of Lincoln on the Rio Bonito, had been a steady friend of Murphy & Dolan's during all the troubles, and his hospitable dwelling was always open to their friends. Hence the Kid and his adherents bore him no good will. So they made a descent on his ranch and got away with eighteen or twenty horses, most of them valuable ones. With their booty, they returned to Sumner and secreted the stock near by.

There was at Fort Sumner at this time a buffalo hunter who had just returned from the Plains, by name John Long or John Mont or John Longmont. He was a six-footer, a splendid shot, and one who coveted the reputation of a "bad man." In reality, he was only a boisterous bully. A day or two after the Kid returned from his raid on Fritz' ranch, Long, in a drunken frenzy, was shooting his revolver so promiscuously up and down the streets of Sumner that the

Billy the Kid

terrified citizens had mostly retired from sight. The Kid, happening to come out of a store, had to spring behind a tree-box in order to avoid the bullets. Here it seemed to Long, to whom the Kid was unknown, was an opportunity for an exhibition of magnanimity.

"Come out, buddy," he shouted, "don't be afraid. I won't hurt you."

"The hell you won't!" replied the Kid. "There's no danger of your hurting anybody unless you do it accidentally. They say you always kill your men by accident."

This retort hit Long hard, as he had killed a man at Fort Griffin, Texas, a short time previously and had saved himself from a furious mob by pleading that it was an accident. He eyed the Kid viciously and asked,

"Where are you from, buddy?"

"I'm from every place on earth but this," responded the Kid, and Long walked sullenly away.

On the following day, Long with several companions was indulging in a big drunk in the little *tendejon* kept by a Jew. As usual, Long was the biggest and loudest talker as well as the drunkenest of the crowd. The Kid entered in company with young Charley Paine, and the two passed to the back of the store. Long hailed them:

"Where are you going?—you damn little son of a b——," said he.

The Kid wheeled quickly and walked up to him with something glistening in his eye which wise men are wont to "let their wisdom fear," and said,

"Who did you address that remark to, sir?"

"Oh," answered Long with a sickly smile, "I was just joking with that other fellow."

"Be very careful," replied the Kid, "how you joke fellows in whose company I happen to be. You will notice that I am the littlest of the two. I am too stupid to understand or appreciate your style of jokes, and if you ever drop another one that hits the ground as close to me as that last, I'll crack your crust. Do you understand?"

Long made no reply; he was completely cowed. The Kid gazed sternly at him for a moment, and then walked carelessly away. The big fighter annoyed him no more. He was killed shortly after at a ranch on the Plains by a Mexican named Trujillo.

The Kid remained at Sumner but a few days; then he, O'Folliard, Bowdre, Wayt, Brown, and Middleton took the horses stolen from Fritz and started up the Rio Pecos with the intention of adding to their herd before they drove them away. They raided Grzelachowski's ranch at Alamo Gordo and other

Billy the Kid

ranches at Juan de Dios and in the vicinity of Puerta
de Luna, forty miles north of Fort Sumner, and in
this way increased their stock of animals to thirty-five
or forty head. Pretty well "heeled" by this time,
they took a course nearly due east and in the direction of the Panhandle of Texas. At Theackey's ranch,
Bowdre sold out his interest in the stolen stock to his
companions, and rejoined Scurlock at Sumner, where he
was employed by Pete Maxwell to herd cattle. The
Kid with the remaining four went to Atascosa on the
Canadian, leaving Fort Bascom on their left and
passing through the plaza of Trujillo.

After the outlaws were gone, the citizens about
Puerta de Luna aroused themselves, and one Fred
Rothe, then a resident of Las Colonias, now of Anton
Chico, raised a party of eight or ten Mexicans, rode
to Fort Sumner to enlist more men, failed to increase
his force, followed the trail of the stolen stock to
Hubbell Springs about twenty-five miles away, got a
good look at both thieves and plunder, but, not being
on speaking terms with the Kid, was too modest to
accost him, and without firing a shot returned to the
river.

The Kid and his band quickly disposed of their ill-
gotten plunder and almost as quickly exhausted the
proceeds at monte tables and saloons. There was little

show to make much of a winning on the Canadian, and the party discussed future movements. Middleton, Wayt, and Brown were tired of the life of danger and privation they had been leading for some months past, and announced their unalterable intention to turn their backs on New Mexico and its bloody scenes forever. They urged the Kid and O'Folliard to accompany them and predicted their tragic end should they remain. All argument failed. Neither party could be persuaded to abandon its design, and they parted company forever. Middleton, Brown, and Wayt were never seen in New Mexico afterwards.

The Kid and O'Folliard returned to Fort Sumner and joined Bowdre and Scurlock. Bowdre continued in the employ of Maxwell but was interested in all the illegal traffic of his friend. The Kid was of the temperament that he must have some person upon whom to concentrate his notice and esteem. Tunstall had been during his life not only his friend but his banker. Now he was dead and amply revenged. Later McSween had supplied the place of Tunstall in the Kid's friendship and interest. Now McSween also was dead. Only John Chisum was left of the trio in whose service he had worked, fought, and killed. So to him the Kid now turned. But Chisum failed to respond to his petitions for assistance—or remuneration, as the Kid chose to term it—and he conceived for Chisum a mortal hatred which he tried to flatter himself was justified by the latter's refusal to countenance him in his lawless career but which was doubtless merely feigned as an excuse to plunder Chisum's vast herds of cattle and horses. So upon returning from the Canadian, the Kid put all his energy into cattle "speculations," Chisum perforce furnishing the capital.

In December, 1878, the Kid and O'Folliard again visited Lincoln. George Kimbrell had been elected sheriff in November and held warrants for both of them. They were arrested and placed in the old jail, which was an insecure building from which they easily made their escape. They returned to Fort Sumner and continued their cattle raids, living "in clover." By his pleasant manners and open-handed generosity, the Kid made himself almost universally popular. Lincoln, with properly exercised authority, would have been a dangerous locality for the Kid, but under existing conditions he was able to flicker around in that vicinity like a moth around a flame. To his daring spirit it was fun to ride through the plaza and salute not only the citizens but the peace officers as well with a cheerful *"Buenos días."*

In the month of February, 1879, the Kid again met

Jesse Evans, and it happened in the plaza at Lincoln. James J. Dolan was bringing in from his ranch a herd of cattle to deliver to the agents of Thomas B. Catron. Dolan had reached a point near Lincoln with his herd, and had gone into the plaza with two of his employees—Jesse Evans and William Campbell. That night these three, in company with Edgar A. Waltz, agent and brother-in-law of Catron, and Billy Matthews, met the Kid and O'Folliard in the street. The meeting was by appointment, and after a few sharp words ended in a reconciliation—all pledging themselves to bury the hatchet and cease their now causeless strife. At the beginning of the interview, Jesse said to the Kid,

"Billy, I ought to kill you for murdering Bob Beckwith."

The Kid replied, "You can't start your lead pump any too quick to suit me, Jesse. I have a hundred causes to kill you."

At this point Dolan and Matthews interfered as peacemakers, and the threatened row was quelled.

The reconciliation effected, all concerned adjourned to a saloon and proceeded to drown old animosities in whiskey. Late in the night a lawyer, named Chapman, arrived in the plaza from Las Vegas. He had been employed by Mrs. McSween to settle up the estate of her deceased husband. It was charged that Chapman was busily engaged in blowing into flame the embers of a dead struggle, and he had succeeded in making many enemies, especially among the Dolan faction. As he was passing the Kid and his companions, all of whom had just issued from the saloon, Campbell, who was chuck-full of bad whiskey and a desire to fight, accosted Chapman insultingly and told him he wanted to see him dance. Chapman replied indignantly. A few words passed between the two and then Campbell shot Chapman dead. The Kid and Jesse were merely witnesses, this being one of the killings in that section in which they did not take a hand. The misfortune of this affair was that two innocent parties were arrested for this crime along with the guilty one. Dolan and Matthews were indicted, tried, and acquitted. Campbell was arrested, placed in the guard-house at Fort Stanton, made his escape, and fled the country. The Kid and Jesse parted that night never to meet again.

NOTE A

There is strong ground for thinking that the Kid should be exonerated for the killing of Bernstein. Accompanying the Kid's gang on this horse-stealing expedition was a young Mexican, said to have been named Sanchez, who was ambitious to be thought a "bad man." In the altercation over the horses, this boy picked up a gun and shot Bernstein.

The Authentic Life of

NOTE B

After the disturbances in Lincoln County had quieted down, and the Kid was making his rendezvous chiefly about Fort Sumner, he seems to have cherished a very definite and implacable grudge against John S. Chisum. There is a persistent tradition that these two met on one occasion and the Kid preferred a claim for several hundred dollars on account of services to Chisum in the Lincoln War. Chisum declined to pay any attention to the demand, and the Kid thereupon declared his intention to steal from Chisum's cattle herds until he had secured what was due him. Some who are friendly to the Kid even point out that most of his cattle stealing from that time on was in truth from the Chisum herds.

The Kid's claim was probably not in the least valid. At no time was he directly in Chisum's employ, and least of all was he in such a relationship during the Lincoln County War. There is no evidence that Chisum provided the sinews of war for the McSween side during the continuance of the feud.

Billy the Kid

CHAPTER XIV

The Kid under Voluntary Arrest at Lincoln—Another Escape from Jail—Continued Wholesale Cattle Stealing—Kills a Texas Desperado Named Grant.

LEAVING Lincoln after his interview with Jesse Evans, the Kid returned to Fort Sumner, and securing some new recruits to his service, he inaugurated a system of plunder which baffled all resistance. A stockowner's only course to secure immunity from loss was to conciliate the Kid and court his friendship, for he always held sacred the property of those he claimed as friends.

There was an attraction in the very danger which attended the Kid's presence in Lincoln. Again, in March, 1879, he, together with O'Folliard, took a trip to that plaza. Upon this occasion they made a showing of complying with the law, and on their arrival, laid away their guns and revolvers. They were again arrested on the old warrants and placed under guard in the house of Don Juan Patron and handcuffed; but otherwise their confinement was not irksome. They were guarded by Deputy Sheriff T. B. Longworth, to whom the Kid had pledged his word that he would make no attempt to escape. Longworth knew him well and trusted him. The Kid and O'Folliard did not betray this trust until they were again placed in jail.

At the house of Patron, they led a gay life with plenty to eat and drink, the best of cigars, and a game of poker with anyone, friend or stranger, who chanced to visit them. The Kid was cheerful and seemingly contented. His hand was small and his wrist large; so it was difficult to keep a pair of handcuffs on him. When a friend entered, he would advance, slip his hand from the irons, stretch it out to shake hands, and remark jokingly, "I don't wish to disgrace you, sir," or, "You don't get a chance to steal my jewelry, old fellow."

On the 21st of March, 1879, Longworth received orders to place the two prisoners in the jail—a horribly dismal hole, unfit for a dog kennel. The Kid said, "Tom, I've sworn I would never go inside that hole again alive."

"I don't see," said Tom, "how either you or I can help it. I don't want to put you there—I don't want to put anyone there. But that's orders and I have nothing to do but to obey. You don't want to make trouble for me?"

The Kid walked gloomily up to the jail door, and

Lincoln, March 15. 1879.

W. H. Bonney.

Come to the house of old
Squire Wilson (not the lawyer) at nine (9)
o'clock next Monday night alone. I don't mean
his office, but his residence. Follow along the
foot of the mountain south of the town, come
in on that side, and knock at the east door.
I have authority to exempt you from prosecution,
if you will testify to what you say you know.

The object of the meeting at
Squire Wilson's is to arrange the matter in a
way to make your life safe. To do that the
utmost secresy is to be used. So come alone.
Don't tell anybody — not a living soul — where
you are coming or the object. If you could trust
Jesse Evans, you can trust me.

Lew. Wallace.

LETTERS THAT PASSED BETWEEN GOVERNOR LEW WALLACE AND BILLY THE KID

This exchange of letters related to the Kid's making a voluntary surrender in 1879. The letters are reproduced through the courtesy of Mr. Lew Wallace, Jr.

San Patricio
Lincoln County
Thursday 20th 1879

General Lew. Wallace;

Sir I will keep
the appointment I made
but be sure and have men come
that You can depend on I am not
afraid to die like a man fighting
but I would not like to be killed
like a dog unarmed, tell Kimbal
to let his men be placed around
the house. and for him to come in
alone; and he can arrest us. all I am
afraid of is that in the Fort we
might be poisined or killed through
a Window at night but You can
arrange that all right. tell the
Comanding Officer to Watch) Let Goodwin
he would not hesitate to do anything
there Will be danger on the road of
Somebody Waylaying us to kill us on the
road to the Fort.

You Will never Catch those fellows on the road Watch Frityos. Captain Bacas, ranch and the Brewery, they Will either go to Secon River or to Picecerille Montians, they Will stay around close untill the scouting parties come in give a Spy a pan of Glasses and let him get on the mountain back of Frityos and Watch and if they are there then will be provisions Carried to them it is not my place to advise you. but I am anxious to have them caught, and perhaps know how men hide from Soldiers, Will You please Excuse me for having so much to say and I still remain Yours Truly

W. H. Bonney

I have't changed my mind send Kimbal to Gulleron just below san Patricio one mile, because Songer and Ballard are, or were great friends of mine Ballard told me to day to leave for you were doing everything to catch me. it was a blind to get me

All Lincoln not to come before Wednesday, I may not be there Sf

Billy the Kid

before going in stopped, saying to Longworth, "Tom, I am going in here because I won't have any trouble with you, but I'd give all I've got if the son of a b—— that gave the order was in your boots."

He passed into the hall and had his cell pointed out to him. The door of unpainted pine was standing open, and taking a pencil from his pocket he wrote on it:

William Bonney was incarcerated first time, December 22nd, 1878; second time, March 21st, 1879, and hope I never will be again.   W. H. BONNEY.

This inscription still stands and was copied by the author in August, 1881. It was suspected that the sheriff knew the stay of the two prisoners in jail would be short and he was tired of feeding them. At all events, they left when they got ready, and the Kid prowled about the plaza two or three weeks, frequently passing up and down in broad daylight with a Winchester in his hand and cursing the sheriff to his heart's content.

In April, they returned to Fort Sumner and resumed depredations on loose stock. This business they followed industriously throughout the sumner and fall. In October of 1879, the Kid with O'Folliard, Bowdre, Scurlock, and two Mexicans rounded up and drove away from Bosque Grande, twenty-eight miles north of

Roswell, one hundred and eighteen head of cattle, which were the property of Chisum. They drove them to Yerby's ranch in his absence, branded them, and turned them loose on the range. This ranch is north of Sumner. They said that Chisum owed them $600 each, for services rendered during the War. They afterwards drove these cattle to Grzelachowski's ranch at Alamo Gordo, and sold them to Colorado beef buyers, telling them that they were employed in settling up Chisum's business. Chisum followed the cattle up, recovered them, and drove them back to his range.

But the Kid had the money and displayed a rare genius as a financier in its disbursement. Out of about $800 he generously gave Bowdre $30, explaining that he did so because he had a family. O'Folliard, he asserted, was a disgrace to the band on account of shabby boots; so he got a new pair as his share. The Mexicans simply got "the shake." There was yet Scurlock to dispose of. The Kid got four or five different parties to go to Scurlock and warn him of the intended arrest of the gang by officers from Lincoln County, and this so scared Scurlock that he borrowed fifty pounds of flour from Pete Maxwell, gathered together his family and household goods, and skipped the country. Thus is Doc Scurlock henceforth lost to

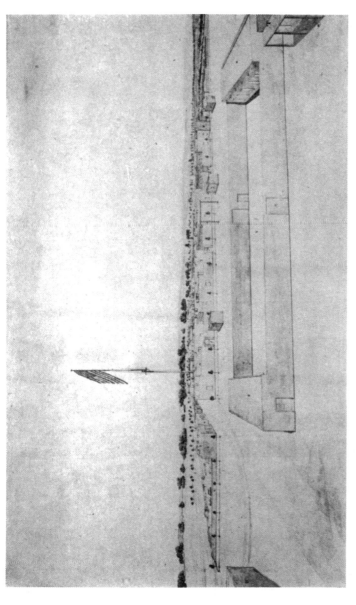

FORT SUMNER, NEW MEXICO—VIEW FROM EAST

This drawing is Fort Sumner in its palmy days when it was a garrison to control the Indians sequestered at Bosque Redondo. The army abandoned it in the early seventies, and much of the original fort, being of adobe construction, fell rapidly into a ruinous condition.

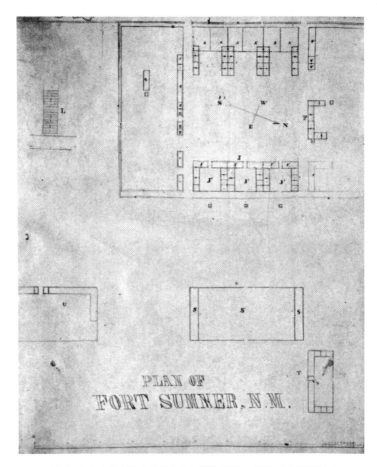

GROUND PLAN OF FORT SUMNER, NEW MEXICO

This plan supplements the drawing opposite. In the time of Billy the Kid, what remained of the old buildings were occupied by Mexicans and Americans. The most prominent in the community were the Maxwells, who had made over for a homestead one of the large buildings built for officers' quarters on the west side of the parade ground. Certain other buildings playing some part in the Billy the Kid episodes may be located through key letters as follows: *C*, quartermaster's storehouse, in which was the room of the friend, Campbell, whom the Kid visited the night of his death and from which he went to Maxwell's house; *T*, the old hospital in which Bowdre's wife lived; *S*, corral.

this history. Out of $800, he got fifty pounds of flour, which still stands charged to profit and loss on Pete Maxwell's books. When asked what he would do with his share, the Kid laughed and said he would endow an insane asylum if he could catch Doc Scurlock.

In January, 1880, a fellow named Joe Grant arrived at Fort Sumner and was straightway cheek by jowl with the Kid and his companions. It afterwards transpired that Grant had heard a good deal of the Kid and sought to win a reputation as a "holy terror," as he termed it, by killing the New Mexico desperado. That Grant had killed his man and was a "bad one," there is no doubt. He disclosed a good deal of his disposition, if not his intention, one day in Sumner by remarking, "I'd like to pick off these fighters and lay them out on their own dung hill. They say the Kid is a bad citizen but I am his loadin' any jump in the road."

The Kid heard this but kept his own counsel. He continued to drink and carouse with Grant every day, and while Grant was swaggering and boasting, the Kid was in his usual jovial humor, but no movement of his companion escaped his wary eye. James Chisum, brother of John S., with three men had been to Canyon Cueva near Juan de Dios north of Fort Sumner, and there recovered a bunch of cattle which had been stolen from their range, it was said, by the Kid. Jim Chisum returned as far as Sumner, arriving there one day about the middle of January, and camped within a mile of the plaza. His party was composed of young Herbert, Jack Finan, and William Hutchison, known on the range as "Buffalo Bill." The Kid, Barney Mason, and Charlie Thomas rode out to Chisum's camp and demanded to look through his herd for the XIX brand. They did so but found no cattle so marked. The Kid then good-naturedly insisted that Chisum and his men should go to Bob Hargrove's saloon and take a drink. There they found Joe Grant viciously drunk. As the party entered, he snatched a fine ivory-handled pistol from Finan's scabbard and put his own in place of it.

The Kid had his eye on him, and remarking, "That's a beauty, Joe," took the pistol from his hand and revolved the chambers. It was his design to extract some of the cartridges, but he found only three in it. So deftly whirling the chambers until the next action would be a failure, he returned it to Grant, who flourished it about and at last said to the Kid, "Pard, I'll kill a man quicker'n you will for whiskey."

"What do you want to kill anybody for?" answered the Kid, "Put up your pistol, and let's drink."

Billy the Kid

During this conversation Grant had passed behind the counter and was knocking decanters and glasses about with his pistol. Thus with the counter between him and the crowd and revolver in hand, it seemed he had the drop on anyone in the room whom he might want. The Kid remarked, "Let me help you break up housekeeping, pard," and drawing his pistol went to knocking the glassware about. Grant continued,

"I want to kill John Chisum, anyhow, the damn son of a b——," and he eyed James Chisum with a wicked glare.

"You've got the wrong pig by the ear, Joe," said the Kid. "That's not John Chisum."

"That's a lie," shouted Grant. "I know better." And turning his pistol full on the Kid, who was smiling sarcastically, he pulled the trigger, but the empty chamber refused to respond. With an oath he again raised the hammer when a ball from the Kid's revolver crashed through his brain and he fell behind the counter. The Kid threw the shell from his pistol and said,

"Unfortunate fool! I've been there too often to let a fellow of your caliber overhaul my baggage. Wonder if he's a specimen of Texas desperadoes."

Someone remarked that perhaps Joe was not killed

and he had better watch out for him. "No fear," replied the Kid. "The corpse is there sure—ready for the undertaker."

He sauntered off unconcernedly, gave orders to a Mexican for the burial, and then calling to "Buffalo Bill" he said: "Bill, stay right with your horse and watch your gun. You had better get your party away as soon as possible. There are some petty larceny thieves in the plaza, who may take a notion to give you a game. I don't like one of the Chisum family and damn few of their friends; but this crowd is here by my invitation and I won't see it handicapped."

The Chisum party got away with the loss of one gun, stolen from their wagon during their absence at the saloon.

Shortly after the killing of Grant, the Kid made a trip down the Pecos, remaining for some weeks in the vicinity of Roswell. The Berrendo settlement, three miles from that place, was his headquarters. He was flush and spent money freely. The Chisum ranch was only about seven miles from Berrendo, and those who knew the Kid best suspected that he harbored the intention of waylaying John Chisum and urging a fight with him. He kept himself pretty full of whiskey, and upon one occasion at Berrendo as he was sitting in front of the saloon watching a covey of snowbirds

Billy the Kid

hopping about, he drew his revolver and remarked to his companions, "Suppose, boys, old John Chisum was a pretty little bird, which he is not, and suppose that pretty little bird sitting on that straw was him. Now if I was to shoot that little bird and hit him anywhere except in the head, it would be murder." And with the words, he fired.

A bystander picked up the dead bird and found its head was shot off. "No murder!" cried the Kid. "Let's give old John another chance," and another bird's head disappeared. He killed several in this manner until at last he hit one in the breast. "I have murdered old John at last," said he. "Let's go and take a drink."

Note A

The murder of Chapman seemed to indicate another outbreak of lawlessness in Lincoln. Governor Wallace, who had tried to terminate the original feud by his proclamation of pardon issued November 13, 1878, promptly came to Fort Stanton and took personal charge of the efforts to stamp out the new appearance of lawlessness. One of his steps towards this end was to induce the Kid, who had been a witness to the Chapman killing, to turn state's evidence. Proof of this is in the following letters, which are on display in the Wallace Study, Crawfordsville, Indiana:

Lincoln, March 15, 1879.
W. H. Bonney,
Come to the house of Old Squire Wilson (not the lawyer) at nine (9) o'clock next Monday night alone. I don't mean

his office, but his residence. Follow along the foot of the mountain south of town, come in on that side and knock at the east door. I have authority to exempt you from prosecution if you will testify to what you say you know.

The object of the meeting at Squire Wilson's is to arrange the matter in a way to make your life safe. To do that the utmost secrecy is to be used. *So come alone.* Don't tell anybody—not a living soul—where you are coming or the object. If you could trust Jesse Evans, you could trust me.

LEW WALLACE.

The Kid must have kept the appointment and learned what plan Governor Wallace had to suggest. That this involved his voluntary surrender is evident from the Kid's reply a few days later:

San Patricio,
Lincoln County,
Thursday, [March] 20th, 1879.

General Wallace,
  Sir:
      I will keep the appointment I made but be sure and have men come that you can depend on. I am not afraid to die like a man fighting but I would not like to die like a dog unarmed. Tell Kimbrell to let his men be placed around the house and for him to come in alone; and he can arrest us. All I am afraid of is that in the Fort we might be poniarded or killed through a window at night but you can arrange that all right. Tell the commanding officer to watch Lt. Goodwin (he would not hesitate to do anything). There will be danger on the road of somebody waylaying us to kill us on the road to the Fort. You will never catch those fellows on the road. Watch Fritzes, Captain Baca's ranch and the Brewery. They will either go to Seven Rivers or the Jacarilla Mountains. They will stay around close until the scouting parties come in. Give a spy a pair of glasses and let him get on the mountain back of Fritzes and watch, and if they are there, there will be provisions carried to them. It

Billy the Kid

is not my place to advise you, but I am anxious to have them caught, and perhaps know how men hide from soldiers better than you. Excuse me for having so much to say and I still remain,

Yours truly,

W. H. BONNEY.

P.S.

I have changed my mind. Send Kimbrell to Guiterez' just below San Patricio one mile because Sanger and Ballard are or were great friends of Campbell's. Ballard told me yesterday to leave for you was doing everything to catch me. It was a blind to get me to leave. Tell Kimbrell not to come before 3 o'clock for I may not be there before.

Apparently the plan was carried out and the Kid submitted to arrest by the new sheriff, George Kimbrell. He was in custody when court convened on the 14th of April, 1878. During that term he pleaded not guilty to the two indictments standing against him, one of these being for the murder of Brady and the other probably being for the murder of Hindman. He also appeared before the grand jury as a witness in the inquiry which resulted in the indictment of Dolan and Campbell for murder and of Jesse Evans as accessory in connection with the killing of Chapman. During this term of court the cases against the Kid were transferred under a change of venue to Dona Ana County, and when the Kid later stated that he was unable to pay for the issuing of the necessary papers, the court ordered that these be issued and served free of cost.

Just how and why the Kid escaped from custody are now very uncertain. Some aver that he became disgusted with the dilatoriness in connection with his cases, and simply left when he had become tired of waiting around in Lincoln. Others say that he became afraid on account of his appearance before the grand jury and felt that there were safer places for him than Lincoln just then. And some hold that he had learned through confidential sources that Governor Wallace would not or could not keep the promise of immunity he had made, and therefore the Kid felt it safer to return to his old reliance on his six-shooter.

The Authentic Life of

The Kid was a witness before the court of inquiry which convened at Fort Stanton in April, 1879, to investigate Col. Dudley's activities with his soldiers during the three days' fight in Lincoln.

Billy the Kid

CHAPTER XV

No event of importance attended the Kid's visit to the Berrendo section, but on his return to Fort Sumner, he enlisted Billy Wilson, Mose Dedrick, Pascal Chaves, Ighenio Salazar, and Señor Mora in an enterprise which had for its object the acquisition of Indian ponies. They went to the Mescalero Apache Indian Reservation and stole forty-eight head from those Indians. The Kid must have become avaricious, as it is said he appropriated thirty head of this lot to his own use and benefit. They were traded off all up and down the Rio Pecos. This expedition was made from Bosque Grande in February, 1880. In May, the Kid, Bowdre, Pickett, and one other accomplice whose name is unknown left Fort Sumner and went in an easterly direction. Near Los Portales they stole a bunch of fifty-four head of beef cattle belonging to cattle owners on the Canadian in the Panhandle of Texas. These they drove to White Oaks, and sold to Thomas Cooper for $10 per head.

They returned to Fort Sumner some time in June with a bunch of horses stolen by them in the vicinity of White Oaks. In July, they stole a bunch of cattle from John Newcomb at Agua Azul (Blue Water), about fifteen miles from Lincoln at the base of Sierra Capitan, branded them, and turned them loose on the range. During the summer they made various successful raids. They drove off ten head of work steers, the property of a Mexican of Fort Sumner, and sold them, together with twenty head more, to John Singer at Las Vegas. The Mexican followed Singer, overtook him near Las Vegas, and recovered his cattle. About the 15th of November, the Kid, O'Folliard, Tom Pickett, and Buck Edwards stole eight head of fine horses from the ranch of A. Grzelachowski at Alamo Gordo, and started in the direction of White Oaks with them. They traded four of them to Jim Greathouse, turned two out on the Cienega del Macho, and kept two for their own use. Of these latter two, one was subsequently shot under the Kid and the other captured at Coyote Springs.

On the night of the 22nd of November, 1880, an attempt was made by unknown parties to get away with some horses of J. B. Bell's, who lived in the southwestern portion of the town of White Oaks. On the following morning the rumor was rife that the Kid

Billy the Kid

and his gang were in camp at Blake's sawmill, near town. On this information Deputy Sheriff William H. Hudgens summoned a posse comprising the following citizens: George Neil, John N. Hudgens, John Longworth, James Carlyle, James S. Redmond, J. P. Eaker, J. W. Bell, and William Stone. This party lost no time in visiting the camp of the outlaws, but found it deserted. They, however, struck the trail and followed it in the direction of Coyote Springs. About five miles from White Oaks the posse met Mose Dedrick and W. J. Lamper riding in the direction of town. These men were known to be friends of the Kid and his band, and it was also known that they had left White Oaks that morning about the same time as the officer's posse. Hudgens suspected that they had been to a rendezvous of the Kid's to give information and convey provisions. On this suspicion he arrested them.

The posse rode on to the vicinity of Coyote Springs, when they were fired upon from a concealed temporary camp of the outlaws; and a horse ridden by John Hudgens, the property of Neil, was killed. The posse promptly returned the fire. The Kid's horse fell dead under him, and after a brief delay, the outlaws fled. On examining the camp, Hudgens found a fine saddle, said to be the property of the Kid, beside the dead body of the horse. They also found an overcoat known to have been worn in White Oaks that morning by Mose Dedrick, and another known to have been the property of Sam Dedrick, brother to Mose. The Kid was known to be without an overcoat, and his friend Sam had doubtless supplied the "much felt want." At all events, the coat was afterwards worn frequently in Sam Dedrick's presence by one of Hudgens' posse, but Dedrick never attempted to lay claim to it. Besides the spoils already named, the sheriff's posse found a considerable quantity of canned goods and other provisions together with a pair of saddle-bags containing useful dry-goods, all of which were known to have been purchases at White Oaks that morning.

Deputy Sheriff Hudgens then returned to town with his party, arriving there about dark. The Kid's crowd had become separated during the mêlée, Cook and Edwards not answering to his roll-call. The Kid and the remnant of his party had not fled very far away from their camp; and as soon as the Hudgens posse had gotten well out of sight, they, too, took the road to White Oaks. Now the pursued became the pursuers. When they reached White Oaks, they made no attempt at depredations, but appeared merely to seek concealment. They rode to the stables and corral

WHERE BILLY THE KID HAD TWO OF HIS BATTLES

Upper, Blazer's Mill, where took place the fight with Buckshot Roberts. The inset shows what remains of the building in which Roberts took refuge. *Lower,* Coyote Springs, near Carrizozo, New Mexico, where was an encounter with the Hudgens' posse.

Billy the Kid

of West & Dedrick, where they all remained out of sight, except the Kid who was bold enough to go about on the main street of the town. As he entered the door of a certain club room with his broad-brimmed hat drawn down over his eyes as a disguise, a man who knew the Kid well and was known by him, started to speak to him; but the Kid stayed his salutation with a warning glance and the quick ejaculation, *"Chicto! compadre* (Hush! partner)."* The Kid kept in the background but bore himself with as much nonchalance as if he were an hourly visitor there.

If anyone else recognized the Kid on this occasion, it was either someone who was not his enemy or someone who feared the consequences of giving the alarm, for the room contained at that time fully one-half of Hudgens' posse, and they were brave men. On the first intimation of the Kid's presence, a bloody carnival would have been inaugurated wherein more than one man would have bit the dust, and though the Kid seemingly bore a charmed life, his escape would have been less than a miracle. There is little doubt that he went to the club room with murder in his heart and the instrument for accomplishing it on his person, but against whom his vengeance was directed can only be surmised. Some unknown person's absence from that room saved his life, as no fear of danger would have stayed the Kid's hand had he found the victim he sought. More than one heart throbbed tumultuously and more than one cheek paled when, the next morning, it was known that the Kid had been in the club room the night before.

On the following night, November 23rd (it was the Kid's birthday), he and his companions rode boldly into White Oaks about 9 o'clock, and seeing Jim Redmond standing in front of Will Hudgens' saloon, fired on him. The night was dark, the shelter of buildings was handy, and no one was hurt. The Kid's party shortly afterwards rode out of town, and on the outskirts came upon Jimmie Carlyle and J. N. Bell, whom Hudgens had left on guard. These two fired on the outlaws, but with no visible effect. On the 24th and 25th of November, the two prisoners, Mose Dedrick and Lamper, who had been taken into custody on the 23rd, were brought before Probate Judge James A. Tomlinson for examination. Lamper was discharged, but Dedrick was placed under bond to secure his appearance before the district court. He immediately skipped the country, and the bond was forfeited.

Another posse was raised by Constable T. B. Longworth on the evening of November 26th. In addition to Longworth, this party consisted of William H.

Billy the Kid

Hudgens, John N. Hudgens, James Watts, John Mosby, James Brent, J. P. Langston, Ed Bonnell, W. G. Dorsey, J. W. Bell, J. P. Eaker, Charles Kelly, and James Carlyle. They left White Oaks that evening, took the Las Vegas road, and proceeded to the ranch of Greathouse & Keck about forty miles distant. Here, from what they believed to be sure information, they expected to find the Kid and his band. They arrived at their destination about 3 o'clock in the morning of the 27th, and erected four breastworks at available points within easy gunshot of the house, behind which they awaited daylight.

The first visible movement at the house was the appearance of the German cook named Steck, who was brought in by Eaker and Brent trembling with fear. He soon told all he knew and disclosed the presence of the Kid's band at Greathouse's. Will Hudgens then wrote a note to the Kid demanding his surrender and sent it to the house by Steck. He soon returned accompanied by Greathouse and they delivered the Kid's reply which was, "You can only take me a corpse." Hudgens told Greathouse that he wanted the Kid, Dave Rudabaugh, and Billy Wilson; but Greathouse simply replied, "If you want them, go and take them." Hudgens then sent word to Billy Wilson requesting him to come out for an interview and promising him that if after the conversation he did not wish to surrender he should be allowed to return to the house unharmed.

Wilson declined to leave the house but said that if he might talk with Jimmie Carlyle perhaps he would conclude to surrender. In his turn he pledged his word that if Carlyle entered the house he would not be detained or hurt. It is generally believed that Wilson would have surrendered if he had not been restrained by the Kid and Rudabaugh against whom there were charges of capital crimes. Hudgens refused to allow Carlyle to go to the house, but Greathouse urged that he be permitted to do so, saying, "Let him go. There will be no harm come to him. I myself will remain here as a hostage, and if he is hurt, let my life answer for the treachery." Nevertheless Hudgens still withheld his consent until Carlyle himself announced his determination to go and see Wilson and, resisting all argument to dissuade him from the step, disarmed himself, and entered the—to him—fatal stronghold.

Greathouse remained outside with the Hudgens posse. The hours passed away, and the anxious friends of Carlyle awaited in vain his re-appearance. It had been discovered that the outlaws were well supplied with whiskey in the house, and conjectures were exchanged as to the effect that condition of affairs might have on the result of the interview. About 2 o'clock in the afternoon, those on the outside were startled by a crash from the shattered glass in one of the windows of the house, and on turning their eyes in that direction, they saw Carlyle leap out of the opening and make a rush for the barricades. Immediately they heard a sharp fusillade of shots from fire-arms within the house, and Carlyle fell dead before he had gotten ten feet from the window.

One word to the memory of poor Jimmie. He was a young blacksmith who had been in the Territory a little more than a year, but in that short time he had made hundreds of friends and not one enemy. He was honest, generous, merry-hearted, quick-witted, and intelligent. His bloody murder excited horror and indignation, and many who had viewed the lawless career of the Kid with some degree of charity, now came to hold him in unqualified execration as the mur-derer of an exceptionally good man and useful citizen.

Longworth had been dispatched to White Oaks for reinforcements and provisions. The posse had been without food and water for more than twenty-four hours and had suffered intensely from cold and expo-sure. They did not deem it practicable to attempt to hold out until Longworth's return, so they went back as far as Hocradle's ranch, about fifteen miles from

White Oaks and twenty-five from Greathouse & Keck's. Greathouse himself they released as they held him by no legal process and as they exonerated him of any complicity with the treachery that had brought about Carlyle's death.

After reconnoitering carefully and convincing themselves that their enemies had returned home, the Kid and his followers left under cover of night. They were all on foot and made direct for the ranch of a confederate a few miles distant. There they got breakfast and left hurriedly in the direction of Anton Chico on the Rio Pecos, twenty-five miles below Las Vegas. In the meantime, Johnny Hurley had raised a posse at Lincoln to reinforce Longworth. He met Longworth's party at Hocradle's ranch, got what information they had, went to the ranch of Greathouse, took the outlaws' trail to the ranch of their confederate where they had taken breakfast, found the birds flown, but burned the ranch, and thus wiped out one rendezvous of the gang. Then this posse returned to Lincoln.

Jim Greathouse did not remain long at his ranch after the Kid and party left. He was next seen at Anton Chico, and it was strongly suspected that he supplied the outlaws with horses there. They were seen one evening near Anton Chico on foot; Greathouse was that day in the plaza; the next morning they were

Billy the Kid

mounted. They took breakfast at Lane's mail station, fifteen miles east of Anton Chico, but they lost no time at the station, taking a southerly direction to Las Cañaditas. The number in the Kid's party was now reduced to three—the Kid, Dave Rudabaugh, and Billy Wilson. At Las Cañaditas, they were joined by Tom O'Folliard, Charlie Bowdre, and Tom Pickett, this doubling their force.

Note A

The generally accepted version of what happened after Carlyle went into the house is as follows: As soon as he had come among the Kid's crowd, all of whom were more or less drunken, they began some rough fun with him. Among other things they insisted that he drink a health to the Kid, and though this must have gone against the grain with Carlyle, he conformed to the demand. After a while the Kid noticed sticking out of Carlyle's pockets one of a pair of gloves he had left behind a day or two before when he had beat a retreat from his camp at Coyote Springs. This recalled the hardships he had undergone in being compelled to walk a long distance in deep snow after their horses had been killed by the Hudgens posse. So snatching the glove from Carlyle's pocket and holding it before his face, the Kid asked,

"Jim, was you with that mob the other day who caused me such a tramp through the snow without food?"

"Yes," was Carlyle's answer.

"Well, then," said the Kid, "come up and take your last drink on this earth, for I am going to blow your light out."

Carlyle obeyed, with the Kid all the while threatening him with his pistol. When he had taken a drink, the Kid told him to say his prayers, while the Kid counted three. No sooner had the word "three" been uttered, than the Kid fired, the bullet striking its mark, which was not Carlyle's head but a tin can hanging on the wall a few inches above his head.

"Well, Jim," was the Kid's remark, "you are worth several dead men yet, ain't you?" and leading the trembling Carlyle to the bar, he insisted on another drink, asking, "You didn't think I would be brute enough to shoot you in such a cruel manner, did you, Jim?"

Carlyle's companions on the outside were alarmed at hearing the shot, thinking that it must indicate that Carlyle had been killed. In order to make sure, a note was sent in by the cook, Steck, which stated that if Carlyle was not back in ten minutes then Greathouse's life would be taken as a forfeit. The Kid's answer was, "Carlyle is safe but we can't give him up just yet. Now remember, if we hear a shot from the outside we will take it for granted that you have carried out your threat by killing Greathouse, and we will have to pay you back by killing your prisoner." This reply was read aloud by the Kid to his companions, and so was heard by Carlyle.

Shortly after the reply had been sent, one of the Hudgens posse (it is said to have been J. P. Eaker) accidentally discharged his gun. Carlyle, hearing the shot and thinking that it could only mean that Greathouse had been killed and that his own death would soon follow in consequence, made a dash to escape, jumping through the window. But before he struck the ground several bullets from the fusillade that followed had pierced his body. He dropped to the ground, crawled a few yards towards his companions, and then fell over dead.

The Kid always expressed great regret for the death of Carlyle, but viewed it as an unavoidable accident. He afterwards stated that his plan was to hold Carlyle prisoner until dark, when his party intended to tie him down and then make their escape.

Billy the Kid

CHAPTER XVI

Garrett Becomes Sheriff of Lincoln County—Barney Mason Made His Auxiliary—Important Clue Incidental to Search for Counterfeiters—Energetic Pursuit of the Kid and His Band Begins.

IN the month of October, 1880, just previous to the events narrated in the last chapter, the author of this history first became in an official capacity actively engaged in the task of pursuing and assisting in bringing to justice the Kid and others of his ilk. As it would be awkward to speak of myself in the third person throughout the rest of this narrative, I shall run the risk of being deemed egotistical and use the first person in the future pages of this book.

In October, Azariah F. Wild, a detective in the employ of the Treasury Department, hailing from New Orleans, La., visited New Mexico to glean information in regard to the circulation of counterfeit money, some of which had certainly been passed in Lincoln County. Mr. Wild sent for me to come to Lincoln to confer with him and assist in working up these cases. I met him there, and in the course of our interview, I suggested that it would be policy to employ a reliable man to join the gang and ferret out the facts. Wild at once adopted the idea, giving me authority to act in the matter according to my judgment. I returned to my home near Roswell and immediately sent to Fort Sumner for Barney Mason whom I had tried and knew I could trust.

Mason came to me at once, but before I could present the matter to him, he told me that he had stopped at Bosque Grande, twenty-eight miles above, at the ranch of Dan Dedrick and that Dan had read him a letter from W. H. West, partner of his brother, Sam Dedrick, in the stable business at White Oaks. The gist of the letter was that West had $30,000 in counterfeit greenbacks and that he intended to take this money to Mexico, there buy cattle with it, and then drive them back across the line. He wanted to secure the services of a reliable assistant whose business would be to accompany him to Mexico, make sham purchases of the cattle as fast as they were bought, receive bills of sale therefor so that in case of detection the stock would be found in the legal possession of an apparently innocent party. West's letter went on to suggest Barney Mason as just the man to assume the role of scapegoat in these nefarious traffickings.

Mason was considerably surprised when he knew that this was the very business about which I had sent for him. Accompanied by Mason, I returned to Lincoln; and Wild, after giving Mason full instructions and finding that he comprehended them, employed him at a stipulated per diem salary and expenses to go to White Oaks and fall in with any proposition which might be made to him by West, Dedrick, or any other parties.

Mason left Lincoln for White Oaks on November 20th. The night of his arrival he went at once to West & Dedrick's stable to look after his horse. Let it be understood that there are three Dedrick brothers —Dan, who lived at this time at Bosque Grande, but was later a partner of Sam at Socorro, being the oldest; Sam, who lived then at White Oaks and was the partner of West, being the next in age; and Mose, the youngest, who was floating promiscuously over the country, stealing horses, mules, and cattle, and who at the time of this writing [1882] is now on the wing, having jumped a bail bond. As Mason entered West & Dedrick's corral, he met the Kid, Dave Rudabaugh, and Billy Wilson. Rudabaugh had killed a jailer at Las Vegas in 1879 while attempting to liberate a friend named Webb. He was on the dodge and had associated himself with the Kid. Billy Wilson had sold some White Oaks property to W. H. West and received in payment $400 in counterfeit money. This he had spent, so it was alleged, and accordingly he, too, was on the dodge. There was no graver charge at that time against Wilson than that of passing counterfeit money, but the murder of Carlyle a few days subsequently, as related in the last chapter, rendered him liable to indictment for complicity in that crime.

Mason was well known to the three outlaws and had always been on friendly terms with them. They addressed him in their usual good-natured manner, the Kid asking what brought him there. Mason's reply intimated that a chance to "take in" a band of horses near by was the cause of his presence. The Kid at once "smelled a rat," and in a consultation shortly afterwards with his companions and Dedrick, wanted to kill Mason then and there. Dedrick however vetoed the plan at once, for he knew it could be dangerous to him and his business. Mason knew J. W. Bell, afterwards my deputy, and so he sought Bell and advised him of the presence of the Kid and his party at the corral. Bell promptly raised a posse of citizens, and then went alone to the stable. He interviewed West, who assured him that those he sought were not there. He then inquired about their horses, and West declared that they had no horses there. That state-

THREE NOTED SHERIFFS OF LINCOLN COUNTY

Left, Pat Garrett; *right,* John W. Poe, who succeeded Garrett; *center,* James Brent, who came a short time after Poe. All three played a part in suppressing the lawlessness of 1877-1881. This picture was taken in 1883 or 1884.

ment, however, was false, as Dedrick and West slipped the horses out to the gang during the night.

Mason remained at White Oaks several days, but owing to the intense excitement caused by the presence of the Kid and his pursuit by the citizens, he did not deem it a fitting time to broach the subject of his visit to West. I had told him to be sure to see me before he started for Mexico and to come to Roswell in a few days at all hazards. He reached my house on the 25th. In the meantime I was daily hearing of the depredations of the Kid and his gang in the vicinity of White Oaks. I had heard that they were afoot and guessed that they would go to Dan Dedrick at Bosque Grande for horses. I sent word to my neighbors, requesting them to meet me at Roswell, five miles from my house, at dark. I imparted my plans to Mason, and he volunteered to accompany me.

We left home in the evening, and when near Roswell, we saw a man riding one horse and leading another. He was going south in the direction of Chisum's ranch. We went on to Roswell and found that this wayfarer had avoided that place, and so we concluded that he was dodging. Knowing that the Kid's party had become separated, we thought he might be a straggler from that band trying to get out of the country.

Mason knew all the Kid's party; so, taking him with me, I pursued and caught up with the supposed fugitive near Chisum's ranch. Mason at once recognized him as Cook, who had fled from the fight at Coyote Springs. We disarmed him, took him back to Roswell, and put him in irons. There he remained in charge of Capt. J. C. Lea for some three or four weeks, and was then sent to the jail at Lincoln, whence he made his escape.

My neighbors had responded to my call, and about 9 o'clock that night I started up the Rio Pecos with a posse consisting of the following citizens: Messrs. Lawton, Mitchell, Mason, Cook, Whetston, Wildy, McKinney, Phillips, Hudson, Ollinger, Roberts, and Alberding. At daybreak we surrounded Dedrick's ranch at Bosque Grande. Here we found two escaped prisoners from the Las Vegas jail; one was Webb who had been sentenced to hang for the killing of a man named Kelleher at Las Vegas, and who had taken an appeal; the other was Davis who was awaiting trial for stealing mules. These two had made their escape in company with three others, two of whom had been killed while resisting re-arrest, and the other had been captured and returned to the jail at Las Vegas. We found nobody else that we wanted; and so, causing Webb and Davis to fall into ranks, we proceeded up

Billy the Kid

the Rio Pecos, arriving at Fort Sumner about daylight on the 27th of November.

Here I received a letter from Capt. Lea detailing further depredations of the Kid and his band about White Oaks together with the killing of Carlyle and the incidents that supervened. From a buckboard driver I gained some further information, and I thereupon determined to leave the prisoners, Webb and Davis, under guard at Sumner and pursue the outlaws. I went to A. H. Smith, a citizen of Sumner, and made inquiries. He assured me that the Kid and his two companions had not yet returned from the vicinity of White Oaks, but that O'Folliard, Bowdre, and Pickett were at Cañaditas, about twenty miles north-east from Fort Sumner, where Bowdre was in the employ of T. G. Yerby. Stopping at Fort Sumner only long enough to get breakfast, I left four of my men in charge of the prisoners, and with the balance started for Las Cañaditas. Ollinger and myself were both commissioned as deputy United States marshals and held United States warrants for the Kid and Bowdre for the killing of Roberts on an Indian Reservation.

CHAPTER XVII

A Hot Chase Over the Prairie After O'Folliard—The Kid's "Castle" at Los Portales—A Parley with Bowdre—Difficulties with San Miguel Officers—Reinforcements from the Canadian.

THE country between Fort Sumner and Las Cañaditas was well known to me, and in order to approach Yerby's ranch unobserved, we took across the prairie, intending to make observations from the surrounding hills through our field glasses. When yet some eight miles distant from the ranch, we discovered a horseman riding in that direction who was evidently coming from another ranch about twelve miles from Fort Sumner and was bound for Las Cañaditas. He was a long distance from us, but, with the assistance of excellent field glasses, we recognized Tom O'Folliard. There was a pass through the hills, unknown to any of my party except myself, which would surely enable us to intercept him if we could get through in time. But it was certainly a "hard road to travel"; it was so overgrown with weeds and brush and encumbered with loose rock that it was almost impassable.

With much difficulty we made our way through the pass and came out on the beaten road within three

146

hundred yards of O'Folliard, who had not before suspected our presence. He was, however, equal to the situation. As soon as he saw us, the splendid animal he was riding sprang away under whip and spur and his Winchester pumped lead fast and furiously. We pursued hotly, but, instead of overtaking him as I had expected, he left us like the wind. He fired twenty-six shots, as he afterwards declared; I fired but three times. There were only Lawton and Mitchell with me, as the others had fallen behind in the almost inaccessible ravine; but these two used their rifles industriously. No harm was done by this fusillade on either side, except that O'Folliard's horse was wounded in the thigh. O'Folliard made a splendid run and a brave horseback fight, reaching the ranch and giving the alarm in time, for when we arrived there the birds had flown to the hills.

We, however, approached the ranch with caution, for we were not sure whether O'Folliard had reached the ranch or not. We knew that, if he had done so and if the Kid's party had elected to remain there, they would give us a fight. I had with me only Lawton, Mason, McKinney, and Roberts, as I had sent Mitchell back to bring up the rear. When we arrived at the ranch, I proposed to divide the force we had and charge on the house. But I was overruled, my companions advising that we await the rest of the posse. When we did walk up to the ranch unopposed, our precautions appeared rather ludicrous to us, for we found only Bowdre's wife and another Mexican woman who hailed our advent with "terror-born lamentations." Our labor was not without its reward, for we captured a pair of mules stolen from a stage company on the Rio Grande by Mose Dedrick and by him turned over to the Kid. We also secured four stolen horses.

We returned to Fort Sumner, stayed one night, and relieving the guard over the two prisoners, Webb and Davis, started for the Kid's stronghold, Los Portales, where he was wont to harbor his stolen livestock. This place was sixty miles east of Fort Sumner, and was the veritable castle so graphically described by newspaper correspondents, with its approaches impassable except to the initiated and inaccessible and impregnable to foes. Here was where romance surrounded the young brigand with more than oriental luxury, blessed him with the loves of female beauties whose charm would shame the fairest tenant of an eastern seraglio, and clothed him in the most gorgeous splendor. It seems cruel to rob this fairy castle of its magnificence, to steal the romance from so artfully woven a tale, but the naked facts are as follows: Los

Billy the Kid

Portales is but a small cave in a quarry of rock, not more than fifteen feet high, lying out and obstructing the view across a beautiful level prairie. Bubbling up near the rocks are two springs of cool clear water capable of furnishing an ample supply for at least one thousand head of cattle. There is no building or corral; all the signs of habitation are a snubbing post, some rough working utensils, and a pile of blankets—"just that and nothing more."

The Kid was supposed to have had about sixty head of cattle in the vicinity of Los Portales, all but eight of which were stolen from John Newcomb at Agua Azul (Blue Water). On our visit we found only two cows and calves and a yearling, but we heard afterwards that the Kid had moved his stock to another spring about fifteen miles east. We had brought no provisions with us and only found some musty flour and a little salt in the cave; so we killed the yearling and banqueted on beef straight while there. The next day we circled the camp but found no more stock. Then we returned to Fort Sumner, the expedition having taken four days.

On our return trip, we took dinner at Wilcox's ranch, twelve miles from the Fort. Wilcox told me that Bowdre was very anxious to have an interview with me in order to see if he would be allowed to make bond in case he came in and gave himself up. I left word with Wilcox for Bowdre to meet me at the forks of the road about two miles from Sumner at 2 o'clock of the following day. He kept the appointment, and I showed him a letter from Capt. J. C. Lea of Roswell, which contained a promise that, if he would change his lawless life and forsake his disreputable associates, every effort would be made to procure his release on bail and to give him an opportunity to redeem himself. Bowdre did not seem to place much faith in these promises, and evidently thought I was playing a game to get him into my power. He did, however, promise to cease all connection with the Kid and his gang. He said he could not help but feed them when they came to his ranch, but he promised that he would not harbor them any more than he could help. I told him that if he did not quit them or surrender, he would be pretty sure to get captured or killed, as we were after the gang and would sleep on their trail until we took them dead or alive.

On my arrival at Fort Sumner, I dismissed the posse, all except Mason, and they returned to Roswell. I hired C. B. Hoadley to convey the two prisoners to Las Vegas. On my arrival at Sumner with them from below on the Rio Pecos where I had found them, I had written to Desiderio Romero, sheriff of San

Billy the Kid

Miguel County, advising him that I had them under guard at Fort Sumner and requesting him to come after them. As I had heard nothing from him, I concluded to take them to Las Vegas myself and get them off my hands. The day we were to start Juan Roibal and two other Mexicans came into Sumner from Puerto de Luna to inquire about the horses of Grzelachowski stolen by the Kid. They returned as far as Gearhart's ranch with us and assisted Mason and myself in guarding the prisoners. At Gearhart's, they took the direct route to Puerto de Luna; and after some delay, we started by the right-hand road. We were only three or four miles on our way when a messenger from Roibal overtook us with the information that a sheriff's posse from Las Vegas was at Puerto de Luna on its way to Fort Sumner after the prisoners. This changed my route, and I took the other road.

We met the Las Vegas posse about eight miles from Puerto de Luna and found it was led by two deputy sheriffs, Francisco Romero and a Dutchman, who *was* a Dutchman. They had arrived at Puerto de Luna with three men in a spring wagon and had there swelled the party of five to twenty-five, all Mexicans except the irrepressible Dutchman. The spring wagon had been discarded, and now they were all mounted. They came toward my small party like a whirlwind of lunatics, their steeds prancing and curveting and the riders with loud boasts and swaggering airs. One would have thought this crowd had taken a contract to fight the battle of Valverde over again, or that an army of ten thousand rebels opposed them instead of two manacled prisoners. At Puerto de Luna, the deputies receipted to me for the prisoners; and as I was turning them over, Webb made a request of me. He said he had but $10 in the world but he would give me that if I would accompany him to Las Vegas and protect him on the journey. He argued that it was my duty to do this inasmuch as I had arrested him and he had surrendered to me rather than to such a mob as this that had come from Las Vegas. I told him that if he looked at the matter in that light and feared for his safety, I would go on, but I, of course, refused to take his money.

While the deputies were gone with the prisoners to have them ironed, I happened to be sitting in the store of A. Grzelachowski, when Juanito Maes, a noted desperado, thief, and murderer, approached me, threw up his hands, and said that having heard I wanted him, he had come to surrender. I replied that I did not know him, had no warrant for him, and did not want him. As Maes left me, a Mexican named Mariano Leiva, the big bully of the town, entered. With his hand on a pistol in his pocket, he walked up to me and said he would like to see any damn Gringo arrest him. I told him to go away and not annoy me. He went out on the porch, but there he continued in a tirade of abuse, all directed against me. I finally went out and told him that I had no papers for him and no business with him. I assured him, however, that, whenever I did, he would not be put to the trouble of hunting me, for I would be sure to find him. With an oath, he raised his left arm in a threatening manner, his right hand still on his pistol. I thereupon slapped him off the porch. He landed on his feet, drew his pistol, and fired without effect. My pistol went off prematurely, the ball striking at his feet; the second shot went through his shoulder. Then he turned and ran, firing back as he went, very wide of the mark.

I entered the store to get my Winchester, when in a few minutes Romero, one of the deputy sheriffs, came in and informed me that I was his prisoner. I brushed him aside and told him I did not propose to submit, at the same time asking the ground of my arrest. He replied that it was for shooting at Leiva and extended his hand for my gun. I told him I had no intention of evading the law, but I would not allow him to disarm me. I added that I did not know what sort of a mob I had struck, for one man had deliberately shot at me; and I therefore proposed to keep my arms and protect myself. Mason, who by this time had come in, picked up his rifle and said, "Shall I cut the damn son of a b—— in two, Pat?" I told him not to shoot, adding that I did not mind the barking of those curs. My friend, Grzelachowski, now interfered in my defense, and the bold deputy retired. The next morning I went before an alcalde, had an examination, and was discharged.

Romero had written to the sheriff at Las Vegas that he had arrested the two prisoners and was on his way up with them. He had also stated in his letter that he had Barney Mason, one of the Kid's gang, in his charge. The sheriff immediately started Romero's brother with five or six men to meet us at Major Hay's ranch. They came in all the paraphernalia of war—if possible, a more ludicrously bombastic mob than the one that had appeared at Puerto de Luna. Threats and oaths and shouts made a pandemonium. The Romero who had just joined us swore that he had once arrested the Kid at Anton Chico, which was a lie out of the whole cloth, although he proved his assertion by his posse. He also bragged that he wanted no weapons to arrest the Kid—all that was needful was for him to get his eyes on the outlaw.

Billy the Kid

Yet it is pretty sure that this poodle would have ridden all night to avoid sleeping within ten miles of an old camp of the Kid's. Rudabaugh once remarked that it only required lightning-bugs and corn-cobs to stampede the officers of Las Vegas or Puerto de Luna.

Before we reached Hay's ranch, I had heard that Frank Stewart, agent for cattle owners on the Canadian River, was at or near Anton Chico with a large party, and was hotly on the trail of the Kid and his band with the determination not merely to recover the stolen stock but also to capture the thieves. On this information I had started Mason to Anton Chico with a message to Stewart. The Las Vegas officers objected strongly to his leaving the posse, as they had by some process of reasoning got it into their heads that Mason was their prisoner, although they had no warrant for him and had made no direct effort to arrest him. I paid no attention to their senseless gabble, except to tell them that Mason would be in Las Vegas nearly as soon as we would and that, if they wanted him then, they could arrest him. A few days afterwards in Las Vegas I pointed Mason out to them, but the officers had changed their minds and did not want him. A few miles from Las Vegas this delectable posse stopped at a wayside *tendejon* to take on a cargo of *aguardiente*. I seized the opportunity to escape their society and rode on alone into town. I was ashamed to be seen with that noisy, gabbling, boasting, senseless, undignified mob whose deportment would have disgusted the Kid and his band of thieves.

Billy the Kid

CHAPTER XVIII

Garrett Tightens the Coils Around the Kid—A Modern Don Quixote
—A Trustworthy Spy—On the Kid's Trail Assiduously.

As Mason and myself had left the direct road from
Fort Sumner to Las Vegas in order to meet the San
Miguel officers at Puerto de Luna, we had by so doing
missed the Kid, Rudabaugh, and Wilson, who were
then on their way to Las Cañaditas, as heretofore related. I had understood that Frank Stewart, the agent
of the Panhandle stockmen, was going down the Pecos
to hunt the Kid, and the message I had sent to him at
Anton Chico by Mason, as related in the last chapter,
was to the effect that I wished to see him before he
started. He responded by coming with Mason and
meeting me at Las Vegas. His party he had sent on
to White Oaks. Stewart, I learned, was planning to
search in the vicinity of White Oaks first, and then,
should he miss the gang, to cut across the mountains,
strike the Rio Pecos below, and follow it up. I
opposed this course because I was sure it would give
the outlaws time to leave the country or find a safe
hiding place. Stewart was readily convinced that his

plan would not work, and about 1 o'clock in the afternoon of the 14th of December, Stewart, Mason, and myself left Las Vegas to overtake Stewart's posse and turn them back.

We stopped at Hay's ranch, eighteen miles from Las Vegas, got supper, and continued our ride. About 1 o'clock at night we fell in with some Mexican freighters, camped with them by the roadside, and slept until daylight. We rode hard until about 9 o'clock on the morning of the 15th, when we hove in sight of Stewart's party. While eating a hearty breakfast, Stewart, who wanted to sound the disposition of his men but did not wish to confide all our plans to them, said,

"Boys, there's a bunch of steers down near Fort Sumner which I am anxious to round up and take in."

Their countenances fell when they learned what he was expecting to seize in the vicinity of Fort Sumner, but some of them were even more dismayed when they learned that a conflict with the Kid and his gang might be on the program, while the others were more than willing to take a hand. Finally Stewart said,

"Do as you please, boys, but there is no time to talk. Those who are going with me, get ready at once. I want nobody that hesitates."

In a moment Lon Chambers, Lee Hall, Jim East,

Billy the Kid

"Poker Tom," "The Animal," and "Tenderfoot Bob" were in the saddle ready to accompany us.

We took a south-westerly direction, aiming to strike the Rio Pecos at Puerto de Luna. The first day we made about forty-five miles and pulled up at a Mexican ranch some fifteen miles north of Puerto de Luna about 9 o'clock that night, where we found entertainment neither for man nor beast. We, however, consoled ourselves with remembrances of buffalo humps we had consumed in days past and feasted on anticipations of good cheer on the morrow.

On the morning of the 16th, we took the road at daylight. It was intensely cold, and some of our party walked, leading their horses, in order to keep their feet from freezing. Between 8 and 9 o'clock we drew up in front of Grzelachowski's store and were cordially welcomed and hospitably entertained. For the sake of our horses, we determined to lay over until the next morning. We spent the day infusing warmth into our chilled bodies through the medium of mesquite root fires and internal applications of liquid fuel. We were entertained by the vaporings of one Francisco Arragon, who was a veritable Don Quixote—with his mouth. Over and over again, he captured the Kid and all his band, each time in questionable Spanish. His weapons were eloquence, fluency, and well-emphasized oaths, inspired by frequent potations of a mixed character. This redoubtable warrior did not take to me kindly, but lavished all his attention and maudlin sentiment on Stewart and Mason, and threw before them the ægis of his prowess and infallibility.

At last he invited my two companions to accompany him to his house, just across the street, where he promised they could regale themselves with rock and rye *ad infinitum*. Little persuasion was necessary to start my friends. The rock and rye was produced, and after two or three libations, Don Francisco opened his combat with the windmills. It was his philosophy that, as they were run by wind, they must be fought by wind, and he launched whole tornadoes against invisible foes. It was evidently the object of this hero to impress the wife of his bosom with his bravery, and he succeeded to such an extent that his raving elicited from her a thousand passionate entreaties that he would stay his dreadful hand and refrain from annihilating the Kid and all his cohorts, thus endangering his own precious life. This was what Arragon was playing for, and if she had failed to exhibit distress and alarm, he would doubtless have hammered her black and blue as soon as he had her alone.

Billy the Kid

And yet her entreaties only redoubled his profane threatenings.

He was eager to get at the bloody desperadoes; he wanted neither me nor any of my party to accompany him; he alone would do all the fighting, would round them up, bring them in, and turn them over to me. He seemed to think Americans were scarce, and he seemingly wanted to save them. He was going to get me all the volunteers I wanted in the morning ten, twenty, thirty. After fighting this long range battle until nearly night, he concluded to start out immediately and bring them in right away. He expected that they would take to shelter when they saw him coming, but he would tear the walls down over their heads and drag them out by the heels. At last, the trio of listeners, Stewart, Mason, and the Mexican's wife, elicited from him a solemn pledge that he would for the time being give the Kid and his followers a few hours' lease of life.

In the morning I thought I would waste a little time and see if I could get this doughty ally to come along with us. Stewart begged of him the privilege of being allowed to go along with him just to see how he made his capture. Arragon said he would be ready at 10 o'clock, and mounting his horse, he rode furiously up and down the streets and the plaza pretending to be enlisting recruits, but secretly dissuading citizens from going. When 10 o'clock arrived we asked him if he was ready. He was not but would be almost immediately. About 2 o'clock, the bold Arragon announced to us that he had no legal right to interfere with the outlaws and declined to accompany us. It was with difficulty I prevented Stewart from roping and dragging him along with us by the horn of his saddle.

We got away from Puerto de Luna about 3 o'clock in the evening with but one recruit—Juan Roibal. Of all the cowardly braggarts in the place, not one could be induced to go when the time came. They were willing to ride in any direction but that in which the Kid might be encountered. I must, however, except two young men, Americans—Charlie Rudolph and George Willson—who did not start with us, having neither horses nor arms, but, ashamed of the pusillanimity of their townsmen, they borrowed horses and arms and overtook us at John Gearhart's ranch, eighteen miles below Puerto de Luna and twenty-five above Fort Sumner. We reached Gearhart's about 9 o'clock on the night of December 17th in a terrible snowstorm from the north-west. We got a lunch, rested a while, and by 12 o'clock were again in the saddle with a ride

BRAZIL-WILCOX RANCH HOUSE

Upper, front view. *Lower,* rear view. Originally the house had
a flat dirt roof.

of twenty-five miles before us which we were determined to make by daylight.

The day before I had started a spy, José Roibal, brother of Juan, from Puerto de Luna to Fort Sumner. He was a trustworthy fellow, who had been recommended to me by Grzelachowski. He had ridden straight through to Fort Sumner without stopping, obtained all the information possible, and on his return reported to me at Pablo Beaubien's ranch, a mile above Gearhart's. His appearance at Fort Sumner had excited no suspicion. He kept his eyes open and his mouth closed; when it was necessary to talk, he pretended he was a sheep-herder looking for strays. He learned that it was certain that the Kid, with five adherents, was at Fort Sumner and that he was decidedly on the *qui vive*. It seemed that George Farnum, a buckboard driver, had told the Kid that Mason and I were on the way down towards Fort Sumner, but both Farnum and the Kid were ignorant of the fact that we were not alone. The Kid and his crowd, it was said, kept horses saddled all the time, and were prepared either to give us a warm reception when we should appear on the scene, or to run, as occasion demanded. After gaining all the information possible without exciting suspicion, José rode leisurely from Fort Sumner, crossing the river on the west. O'Folliard and Pickett followed him across the river, and asked him who he was, what his business was, etc. He replied that he was a herder and was hunting stray sheep. This satisfied his questioners, and they allowed him to depart.

After the Kid, O'Folliard, Bowdre, Rudabaugh, Wilson, and Pickett had all met at Las Cañaditas, they had gone directly to Fort Sumner, and were putting in a gay time at cards, drinking, and dancing. The Kid had heard of our capture of the mules and other stolen stock at Yerby's ranch, and was terribly angered thereat. The gang squandered many precious hours in cursing me and threatening me with bloody death. The Kid had written to Capt. Lea at Roswell that if the officers of the law would give a little time and let him alone until he could rest up his horses and get ready, he would leave the country for good. But he added threateningly that, if he was pursued or harassed, he would start a bloody war and fight it out to the fatal end.

With all this information from our faithful spy, we left Gearhart's ranch about midnight and reached Fort Sumner just before daylight. I made camp a little above the plaza, then took Mason and went prospecting. We understood that the outlaws kept their horses when in Fort Sumner at A. H. Smith's corral, and

Billy the Kid

we first visited him. We found that their horses were not there; then we awakened Smith and learned from him that they had left after dark the night before. We all turned in at Smith's except Mason, who went to the house of his father-in-law. He came back, however, immediately with the news that he had heard the Kid and his gang were in an old deserted building near by. This report served to excite us, rouse us out of bed, and disappoint us, as there was no one at the house designated. We concluded perforce that we would possess our souls in patience until daylight.

CHAPTER XIX

Garrett Lays a Trap at Fort Sumner for the Kid's Party—O'Folliard Its Victim—The Kid and His Other Accomplices Escape—Renewed Pursuit of the Band.

ON the morning of the 18th of December, before anyone was stirring in the plaza of Fort Sumner, I left our party with the exception of Mason in concealment, and started out to make observations. I met a Mexican named Iginio Garcia in my rounds, whom I knew to be a tool of the Kid's, and I spoke to him. I warned him not to betray my presence to any of the Kid's gang and not to leave the plaza. He represented that he had urgent business down the river but assured me that he would keep my presence a secret. I consented for him to go, as it didn't matter much. If the Kid and his associates found out I was there, they would labor under the impression that my only support in the engagement would be Mason, and perhaps a Mexican or two. The fact of the presence of Stewart and his party I felt sure had not been betrayed to anyone. Garcia lived twelve miles south of Fort Sumner, and started in that direction.

A day or two previous to these events, A. H. Smith

Billy the Kid

had sent Bob Campbell and José Valdez to Bosque Grande to drive up a bunch of milk cows which he had bought from Dan Dedrick. Garcia happened to meet these two near his home. He knew that Campbell was a friend and an accomplice of the Kid and that Valdez was, at least, a friend. He told them I was in Fort Sumner, and they immediately turned the cows loose and separated. Campbell at once went to a camp close by, hired a Mexican boy, and sent him to the Kid with a note. The Kid and his gang were then at the ranch of Erastus J. Wilcox, twelve miles east of Sumner.

Valdez rode into Sumner, and there, when I met him, I inquired if he had seen Garcia. He said he had seen him at a distance but had not spoken to him. I asked no further questions, as I was convinced I would get no word of truth from him. On receipt of Campbell's note, the Kid sent Juan, a stepson of Wilcox, to the Fort to see how the land lay and with instructions to return and report as soon as possible. Wilcox and his partner, Brazil, were law-abiding citizens, and subsequently rendered me invaluable assistance in my efforts to capture the gang. Seeing Juan in the plaza, I suspected his errand, accosted him, and found my surmise was correct. After a little conversation I concluded that I could fully trust him; and when I made known my business to him he promised faithfully

167

to follow my instructions. From him I gathered the following information about the Kid's movements.

The Kid and all his band were intending to come to Fort Sumner the next day in a wagon with a load of beef. That morning, however, the Kid had received by a Mexican boy a note from Bob Campbell wherein Bob told how he and Valdez met Garcia and how Garcia had notified them of my presence in Sumner. So from this I knew that Valdez had lied to me. This note had disarranged the Kid's plans. He had sent Juan in to try to learn something of my movements, the number in my posse, etc. I asked Juan if he would work with me to deceive the outlaws. He said he would do anything I told him. Thereupon I left him and went to Valdez. I made the latter write a note to the Kid saying that all my party and I had gone to Roswell and there was no danger. I then wrote a note to Wilcox and Brazil, stating that I was at Fort Sumner with thirteen men, that I was on the trail of the Kid and his gang, and that I would never let up until I caught them or ran them out of the country. I closed with the request that they coöperate with me. When Juan had finished his business in the plaza and came to me, I gave him the two notes, warning him not to get them mixed.

The Kid and his party were impatiently awaiting

Billy the Kid

Juan's return. They read Valdez' note eagerly—
then shouted their scorn at my timidity, saying that this
news was too good for them; that they had intended
to come in after me anyhow; that they had a great
notion to follow me and my party; that if they could
kill me they would not be further molested; and that
if we had not run away they would have "shot us up
a little" and set us on foot. Juan was discreet, and
when opportunity arose, he gave the other note to
Wilcox.

I was confident that the gang would be in Fort
Sumner that night and made arrangements to receive
them. There was an old hospital building on the
eastern boundary of the plaza—the direction from
which they would come. The wife of Bowdre occupied one of the rooms of the building, and I felt
sure they would pay their first visit to her. So I
took my posse there, placed a guard about the house,
and awaited the game. They came fully two hours
before we expected them. We were passing away the
time playing cards. There were several Mexicans in
the plaza, some of whom I feared would convey information to the gang, as I had them with me in custody. Snow was falling on the ground, the fact of
which increased the light outside. About eight o'clock
the guard cautiously called from the door,

"Pat, some one is coming!"

"Get your guns, boys," said I. "No one but the men we want would be riding at this time of night."

With all his reckless bravery, the Kid had a strong infusion of caution in his composition when he was not excited. He afterwards told me that as they approached the building that night he was riding in front with O'Folliard. As they rode down close to our vicinity, he said a strong suspicion arose in his mind that they might be running into unseen danger.

"Well," said I, "what did you do?"

He replied—"I wanted a chew of tobacco bad. Wilson had some that was good and he was in the rear. I went back after tobacco, don't you see?" and his eyes twinkled mischievously.

One of the Mexicans followed me out, and we joined the guard, Lon Chambers, on one side of the building, while Mason with the rest of our party went around the building to intercept them should they try to pass on into the plaza. In a short time we saw the Kid's gang approaching, with O'Folliard and Pickett riding in front. I was under the porch and close against the wall, partly hidden by some harness hanging there. Chambers was close behind me, and the Mexican behind him. I whispered, "That's him." They rode on up until O'Folliard's horse's head was under the porch. When I called "Halt!" O'Folliard reached for his pistol, but before he could draw it, Chambers and I both fired. His horse wheeled and ran at least a hundred and fifty yards. As quick as possible I fired at Pickett, but the flash of Chambers' gun disconcerted my aim, and I missed him. But one might have thought by the way he ran and yelled that I had a dozen bullets in him. When O'Folliard's horse ran with him, he was uttering cries of mortal agony; and we were convinced that he had received a death wound. But he wheeled his horse, and as he rode slowly back, said, "Don't shoot, Garrett. I am killed."

Mason, from the other side of the house where he had been stationed, called out, "Take your medicine, old boy; take your medicine," and was going to O'Folliard's assistance. But fearing that it might be a feint and that O'Folliard might attempt revenge on Mason, I called out a warning to the latter to be careful how he approached the wounded man. Then I called to O'Folliard to throw up his hands, adding that I would give him no chance to kill me. He replied that he was dying and couldn't throw up his hands, and begged us to take him off his horse and let him die as easy as possible. Holding our guns down on him, we went up to him, took his gun out of the scabbard, lifted him off his horse, carried him into the house, and laid him down. Then taking off his pistol, which was full-cocked, we examined him and found that he was shot through the left side just below the heart, his coat having been cut across the front by a bullet.

During this encounter with O'Folliard and Pickett, the rest of our party on the other side of the house had seen the Kid and the others of his gang. My men had promptly fired on them and killed Ruda-baugh's horse, which, however, ran twelve miles with him to Wilcox's ranch before the animal died. As soon as our men fired, these four ran like a bunch of wild Nueces steers. They were, in truth, completely sur-prised and demoralized.

As soon as the outlaws had disappeared Mason came around the building just as O'Folliard was re-turning, reeling in his saddle. After we had laid him down inside, he begged me to kill him, saying that if I was a friend of his I would put him out of his misery. I told him I was no friend of his kind who tried to murder me because I tried to do my duty; and I added that I did not shoot at my *friends* as he had been shot. Just then Mason entered the room again. O'Folliard at once changed his tone and cried, "Don't shoot any more, for God's sake. I am already killed." Mason again told him to take his medicine. O'Folliard replied, "It's the best medicine I ever took." He also asked Mason to tell McKinney to write to his grandmother in Texas and inform her of his death. Once he exclaimed, "Oh, my God, is it possible that I must die?" I said to him just before he died, "Tom, your time is short." He answered, "The sooner the better; I will be out of pain then." He blamed no one and told us who had been in the Kid's party with him. He died in about three quarters of an hour after he was shot.

Pickett, who was riding by O'Folliard's side, was unhurt but he was nearly scared to death. He went howling over the prairie yelling bloody murder and was lost until the next night. He ran his horse to exhaustion and then took out on foot, reaching Wilcox's ranch about dark. He had run his horse fully twenty-five miles in a north-easterly direction before the animal gave out and then had to walk twelve or fifteen miles to the ranch. There he hid himself in a haystack and remained there crouching in fear and trembling until he saw his companions ride in from the hills.

The Kid, Rudabaugh, Bowdre, and Wilson first went to Wilcox's ranch where Rudabaugh got another horse. Then they lost no time in going to the hills from which they watched the ranch and the surrounding country all the next day with their field glasses.

At dark they rode back to the house, when Pickett showed himself. It must have been amusing to witness this fellow's sudden change from abject cowardice to excessive bravado as soon as he realized he was actually alive and unharmed and had friends within reach to whom he could look for protection. He swaggered about and blew his own horn somewhat in this strain: "Boys, I got that damn long-legged fellow that hollered 'halt.' I had my gun lying on my saddle in front of me and just as he yelled I poured it into him. Oh, I got him sure."

The gang now reduced to five remained at Wilcox's ranch that night, depressed and disheartened. After a long consultation they concluded to send some one to Fort Sumner the next morning to spy out the lay of the land. They took turns at standing guard throughout the night to prevent surprise, and the next morning sent Wilcox's partner, Brazil, to the plaza. They had been made suspicious of treachery on the part of Wilcox and Brazil when they were so effectually surprised at the old hospital building, but had been entirely reassured by them after returning to the ranch.

Billy the Kid

CHAPTER XX

The Kid's Gang Trapped at Stinking Spring—Death of Bowdre—
The Kid's Plan of Escape Checkmated by Garrett's Marksmanship—Surrender of the Kid and Remnant of His Gang.

BRAZIL came to me at Fort Sumner on the morning of the 20th of December. He described the condition of the crestfallen band of outlaws and said they
had sent him in to gather news and report to them.
I told him to return, and, as a ruse, to tell them that
I was at Sumner with only Mason and three Mexicans and that I was considerably scared up and wanted
to get back to Roswell but feared to leave the plaza.
Brazil remained in town until the next day; then, when
he was ready to start, I told him that, if he found the
gang still at the ranch when he arrived there, he should
remain; but if they had left, or should leave after his
arrival, he was to come and report to me. I had
it understood further between us that, if he did not
come to me before two o'clock in the morning, I
would start for the ranch, and if I did not meet him
on the road, I would feel sure that the Kid's gang were
still at the ranch. Brazil went home and almost immediately returned, reaching Sumner about 12 o'clock
in the night.

175

There was snow on the ground, and it was so desperately cold that Brazil's beard was full of icicles. He reported that the Kid and his four companions had taken supper at Wilcox's, then mounted their horses and departed. My party and I all started for the ranch immediately. I took the precaution to send Brazil ahead to see whether the gang had returned, while with my posse I took a circuitous route by Lake Ranch, a mile or two off the road, thinking they might be there. We reached the ranch, surrounded the house, found it vacant, and rode on towards Wilcox's. About three miles from there we met Brazil, who reported that the outlaws had not returned and showed me their trail in the snow.

After following this trail a short distance, I was convinced that they had made for Stinking Spring, where there was an old deserted house, built by Alejandro Perea. When within a half mile of the house, we halted and held a consultation. I told my companions that I was confident we had them trapped, and cautioned them to preserve silence. We moved quietly in the direction of the house until we were only about four hundred yards distant; then we divided our party, leaving Juan Roibal in charge of the horses. Taking one-half of our force with me, I circled the house. I found a dry arroyo, and by taking advantage

WHERE BILLY THE KID SURRENDERED TO GARRETT

Upper, the site of the rock house near Stinking Spring, where the Kid had "holed up" when captured. The inset, although not a picture of the original house, serves to give an idea of what it was like. *Lower*, what remains to-day of the rock house—merely stones outlining the foundation.

Billy the Kid

of its bed we were able to approach pretty close. Stewart, with the rest of the posse, found conceal- ment on the other side within about two hundred yards of the building. We could see three horses tied to the porch and rafters of the house, and knowing there were five in the gang and that they were all mounted when they left Wilcox's, we concluded that they must have led two horses inside. There was no door to the house—just an opening where a door had once been. I had a messenger creep around to Stewart and propose that as the Kid's gang were surely there we stealthily enter the house, cover them with our guns, and hold them until daylight. Stewart did not view the suggestion favorably, although Lee Hall was de- cidedly in favor of it. So, shivering with cold, we awaited daylight or some movement on the part of the inmates of the house.

I had a perfect description of the Kid's dress, especially his hat. I had told all the posse that if the Kid made his appearance it was my intention to kill him, for then the rest would probably surrender. The Kid had sworn that he would never give himself up a prisoner, and would die fighting even though there was a revolver at each ear, and I knew he would keep his word. I was in a position to command a view of the doorway, and I instructed my men that when I brought up my gun they should all raise theirs and fire. Before it was fully daylight, a man appeared at the entrance with a horse's nosebag in his hand, and I took him to be the Kid. His size and dress, especially the hat, corresponded exactly with the description I had been given of the Kid. So I gave a signal by bringing my gun to my shoulder; my men did likewise and seven bullets sped on their errand of death.

Our victim was Charlie Bowdre. He turned and reeled back into the house. In a moment Wilson called to me from the house and said that Bowdre was killed and wanted to come out. I told him to come out with his hands up. As he started, the Kid caught hold of his belt, drew his revolver around in front of him and said, "They have murdered you, Charlie, but you can get revenge. Kill some of the sons of b———s before you die." Bowdre came out with his pistol still hanging in front of him, but with his hands up. He walked unsteadily towards our group until he recognized me; then he came straight to me, motioning towards the house, and almost strangling with blood, said, "I wish—I wish—I wish—" then in a whisper, "I am dying!" I took hold of him, laid him gently on my blankets, and he died almost immediately.

Billy the Kid

As I watched in the increasing daylight every movement about the house, I shortly saw a movement of one of the ropes by which the horses were tied, and I surmised that the outlaws were attempting to lead one of the horses inside. My first impulse was to shoot the rope in two, but it was shaking so that I was confident I would only miss. I did better than I expected, for just as the horse was fairly in the door opening, I shot him and he fell dead, partially barricading the outlet. To prevent another attempt of this kind, I shot in two the ropes which held the other horses and they promptly walked away. But the Kid and his companions still had two horses inside the house, one of them the Kid's favorite mare, celebrated for speed, bottom, and beauty. I now opened a conversation with the besieged, the Kid acting as their spokesman. I asked him how he was fixed in there.

"Pretty well," answered the Kid, "but we have no wood to get breakfast with."

"Come out," said I, "and get some. Be a little sociable."

"Can't do it, Pat," replied the Kid, "business is too confining. No time to run around."

"Didn't you fellows forget a part of your program yesterday?" said I. "You know you were to come in on us at Fort Sumner from some other direction, give us a square fight, set us afoot, and drive us down the Pecos."

Brazil had told me that, when he took the information to the Kid that I had only Mason and three Mexicans with me at Sumner and was afraid to leave for home, the Kid had proposed to come and "take me in." Bowdre, however, had objected to the attempt, and the idea was abandoned. My banter now caused the Kid to catch on to the fact that they had been betrayed, and he became very reticent in his subsequent remarks.

Those in our party were becoming very hungry, and, getting together in one group, we arranged to go to Wilcox's ranch for breakfast. I went first, accompanied by one-half of the other men. The distance was only about three miles. When we reached there, Brazil asked me what news I brought. I told him that the news was bad; that we had killed the very man we didn't want to kill. When he learned it was Bowdre, he said, "I don't see why you should be sorry for having killed him. After you had that interview with him the other day, and was doing your best to get him out of his trouble, he said to me riding home, 'I wish you would get that son of a b—— out to meet me once more. I would just kill him and end all this trouble!' Now, how sorry are you?" I made ar-

Billy the Kid

rangements with Wilcox to haul out to our camp some provisions together with wood and forage for our horses. I had no way to tell how long the outlaws might hold out, and I concluded I would make it as comfortable as possible for myself and the boys. The night previous Charlie Rudolph had frozen his feet slightly. When I and those who had gone with me returned, Stewart and the balance of the boys went to breakfast.

About three o'clock in the afternoon the gang turned loose the two horses from the inside. We picked them up as we had the other two. About four o'clock the wagon arrived from Wilcox's with the provisions and wood, and we built a rousing fire and went to cooking. The odor of roasting meat was too much for the famished lads who were without provisions. Craving stomachs overcame brave hearts. Rudabaugh stuck out from the window a handerchief that had once been white and called to us that they wanted to surrender. I told them they could all come out with their hands up if they wanted to. Rudabaugh then came out to our camp and said they would all surrender if I would guarantee them protection from violence. This, of course, I did readily. Rudabaugh then returned to the house where he and the others held a short consultation. In a few minutes all of them

—the Kid, Wilson, Pickett, and Rudabaugh—came out, were disarmed, given their supper, and started in our custody to Wilcox's. Brazil, Mason, and Rudolph I sent back from the ranch with a wagon after the body of Bowdre. They brought the corpse down to Wilcox's ranch, and, after a short stay, my party and I started for Fort Sumner, getting there before night. We turned Bowdre's body over to his wife, put irons on the prisoners, and by sundown Stewart, Mason, Jim East, "Poker Tom," and myself started for Las Vegas with our prisoners.

During the trip the Kid and Rudabaugh were cheerful and gay, Wilson somewhat dejected, and Pickett was badly frightened. The Kid said that if they had succeeded in leading the three horses, or two of them, or even one of them, into the house he and his crowd would have made a break and got away. He said also that he alone would have made a target out of himself until his mare could carry him out of the range of our guns or we had killed him—all of which might have been done had it not been for the dead horse barring his way. He said he knew his mare would not try to pass that body of a dead horse, and if she had tried to do so, she would have probably knocked the top of his head off against the lintel of the doorway. While at Fort Sumner the

THE OLD COURTHOUSE IN LINCOLN FROM WHICH THE KID ESCAPED

Originally this was the store of L. G. Murphy & Co., but by about 1880 it had been bought by the county. Garrett selected for the Kid's confinement the upstairs corner room in the left end of the building. Foliage conceals in the picture the front window of this room, but the side window can be seen. At that time the stairways to the balcony had not been added to the building.

Billy the Kid

Kid had made Stewart a present of his mare, re-marking in his usual joking way that he expected his business would be so confining for the next few months that he would hardly find time for horseback exercise.

We reached Gearhart's ranch with our prisoners about midnight, rested until eight in the morning, and reached Puerto de Luna at two o'clock in the afternoon on Christmas Day. My friend Grzelachowski gave us all a splendid dinner. My ubiquitous Don Quixote Arragon proffered to me again his invaluable services together with those of his original mob, which I respectfully declined. With a fresh team we got away from Puerto de Luna about four o'clock; but we had not travelled far before our wagon broke down and we were compelled to borrow one of Captain Clancy. We managed, however, to reach Hay's ranch in time for breakfast.

At two o'clock in the afternoon, December 26th, we reached Las Vegas and through a crowd of citizens made our way to the jail. Our objective point was the Santa Fe jail, as there were United States warrants against all our prisoners except Pickett. We intended to leave him at Las Vegas, but we proposed to go on with the other three to Santa Fe the next morning, although we expected, and so did Rudabaugh himself, that the authorities at Las Vegas would insist on holding him for the killing of the jailer. We had made a promise to Rudabaugh that we would take him to Santa Fe and we were determined to do it at all hazards. So Stewart went before an alcalde and made oath that we were holding this prisoner on a United States warrant; this affidavit and our warrant, we believed, would enable us to hold Rudabaugh as our prisoner and take him to Santa Fe.

Billy the Kid

CHAPTER XXI

Garrett in Defense of His Prisoners Stands Off a Mob at Las Vegas
—The Kid in Jail at Santa Fe—Trial and Conviction of the
Kid at Mesilla—The Kid Under a Death-watch at Lincoln.

ON the morning of December 27th, I had fresh
irons placed on the Kid, Rudabaugh, and Wilson. As
Michael Cosgrove, the mail contractor carrying the
mail from Fort Sumner to Roswell, was well acquainted
in Santa Fe, I induced him to accompany me there
with the prisoners, and I therefore released two of
my guards, starting with only Cosgrove, Stewart, and
Mason. After breakfast we went to the jail for our
prisoners. They turned over the Kid and Wilson to
us and we handcuffed them together. Then we demanded Rudabaugh, but they refused to give him up,
saying that he had escaped from that jail and that he
was wanted for a murder committed in Las Vegas.
I argued with them that my right to the prisoner
outranked theirs inasmuch as I was a deputy United
States marshal and had arrested Rudabaugh for an
offense against the laws of the United States and
was not supposed to be cognizant of any other offense
or arrest. I insisted that I was responsible for him

185

as my prisoner and pressed in no uncertain terms my intention to have him. Stewart drew his affidavit on them and they at last turned Rudabaugh over to us.

We had been on the train with our three prisoners but a few minutes when we noticed that a good many Mexicans scattered through the crowd were armed with rifles and revolvers and seemed considerably excited. Stewart and I concluded that their object was to take Rudabaugh off the train. I asked Stewart whether we should make a fight for it if such an attempt was made. He said we would, of course, do so; and I replied, "Let's make a good one." We felt sure that they intended to mob Rudabaugh then and there, and for that further reason were unwilling to give him up. He acknowledged that he was afraid of them, and we were moreover under pledge to protect him and take him to Santa Fe. Stewart guarded one door of the car and I the other. These armed ruffians crowded about the car, but none of them made a formal demand for Rudabaugh or stated their business. Deputy Sheriff Romero, brother of the sheriff, who had so distinguished himself when I brought Webb to him at Hay's ranch, headed a mob of five, who approached the car platform where I was standing, and flourished their revolvers. One of them said, "Let's go right in and take him out of there," and with that they began to push the deputy up the car steps, while the others crowded after him. I merely requested them in my mildest tones to get down, and they slid to the ground like a covey of hard-back turtles off the banks of the Pecos. They did not seem so much frightened as modest and bashful.

Rudabaugh was of course excited; the Kid and Wilson seemed unconcerned. I told all three not to be uneasy, for we intended to make a fight if the mob tried to enter the car; and I added that, if the fight came off, I would arm them and let them take a hand. The Kid's eyes glistened as he said, "All right, Pat. All I want is a six-shooter." Then, as he looked out at the crowd, he remarked, "There is no danger though. Those fellows won't fight." He was correct in his observation, for those in the mob were evidently weakening and all they wanted was for some one to coax them to desist so it would not look like a square backdown. Some influential Mexicans began to reason with them and they quickly subsided. We were detained by them about three-quarters of an hour. I understood afterwards that they had covered the engineer with their guns and threatened him if he moved the train. One of the railroad officials had thereupon warned them of danger from the law for detaining the United States mail. Finally Mollay, a deputy United States marshal who had had some railroad experience, mounted the cab and pulled the train out.

I had telegraphed to Charles Conklin, deputy United States marshal at Santa Fe, and when the train arrived, I found him at the depot waiting for us. I turned the prisoners over to him on the 27th of December, and he placed them in the Santa Fe jail. While they were there, they made an attempt to escape by digging a hole through the adobe walls, hiding the dirt under their bedding. This attempt was, however, frustrated through the vigilance of the officials. Rudabaugh was tried and convicted for robbing the United States mail, but no sentence was passed. Then, on demand of the territorial authorities, he was taken to San Miguel County, tried for the murder of the jailer, convicted, and sentenced to be hung. He took an appeal, and while confined in the Las Vegas jail awaiting a new trial, he made his escape. Billy Wilson was twice arraigned for passing counterfeit money, first at Mesilla and then at Santa Fe, but he has not as yet [1882] had a trial. Should he clear himself of this charge, he still would be in jeopardy for complicity in the murder of Carlyle.

The Kid and Wilson were taken from Santa Fe to Mesilla under charge of Tony Neis, a deputy United States marshal, where the Kid was tried at the March,

BUILDING AT MESILLA, NEW MEXICO, IN WHICH BILLY
THE KID'S TRIAL AND CONVICTION TOOK PLACE.

The first side door indicates the room in which Judge Brady held
court. In later times the building became the well-known Elephant
Saloon, a fact which explains the curious wall decorations.

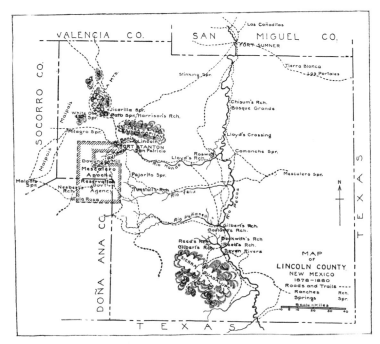

MAP OF LINCOLN COUNTY, NEW MEXICO

This map is intended to show most of the places with which Billy
the Kid was connected. Chisum's Spring River Ranch does not appear, but can be located as a few miles south of Roswell. The Stinking Spring shown was not the one near which the Kid surrendered
to Garrett. That one was located about fifteen miles east of Fort
Sumner.

Billy the Kid

1881, term of the District Court, first for the murder of Roberts at the Mescalero Apache Indian Agency in March, 1878. Judge Bristol, who presided at the trial, assigned Judge Ira E. Leonard, of Lincoln, to defend the Kid, and the outcome of the trial was that he was acquitted. He was again tried at the same term of court for the murder of Sheriff Brady at Lincoln on the 1st of April, 1878, the outcome this time being a conviction. Judge Bristol sentenced the Kid to be hanged on the 13th of May, 1881, at Lincoln. He was brought from Mesilla to Lincoln by Deputy Marshal Robert W. Ollinger and Deputy Sheriff David Woods of Dona Ana County, and turned over to me by them at Fort Stanton, nine miles west of Lincoln, April 21, 1881.

Lincoln County did not then have a jail that would hold a cripple. The county had just purchased the large two-story building, formerly the mercantile house of Murphy & Dolan, for use as a public building, but a new and secure jail had not been constructed. Hence I was obliged to keep the Kid directly under guard all the time. For this duty I selected my Deputy Sheriff, J. W. Bell, and Deputy Marshal Robert W. Ollinger, and chose as a guard-room one of the rooms in the second story of the county building, separate and apart from the quarters given the other prisoners. This room was at the north-east corner of the building, and in order to reach the only door leading into it, a person had to pass from a hall and through another large room. There were two windows—one on the north, opening upon the street, and the other on the east, opening upon a large yard which ran east a hundred yards or more and projected into the street twelve or fourteen feet beyond the north, i.e., the front, walls of the building.

At the projecting corner of the yard and next to the house on the north-west was a gate which opened into a path running along the east end of the building to the south, i.e., the rear, wall, where was a smaller gate opening into a corral at the rear of the house. Inside this corral and at the south-west corner of the building was a door leading into a small hall and broad staircase, which was the only means of access to the second story. A person ascending this stairway would first face north and ascend five or six steps; he would then reach a square landing, and turning at right angles and facing the east, he would ascend twelve or fourteen steps, thus reaching the hall which extended through the building from north to south.

If the person now turned to his right, he would find two doors, one on the east side of the hall and the other on the west. That on the east side opened into a room

Billy the Kid

at the south-east corner which was used as a place for keeping our surplus arms. If, however, at the head of the stairs, a person turned to the left, he would find two other doors, one at each side of the hall, and still another door at the north end, this last door opening upon a balcony. The door on the west side of this part of the hall led into a room which I at that time used for the confinement of prisoners. The door on the east side opened into a large room which I used as an office. In the east wall of this room was a door which led into the north-east room I had selected as the one in which to confine the Kid under guard. The necessity of this description will soon be understood by the reader, whether the description is lucid or not.

During the few days the Kid remained in confinement, I had several conversations with him. He appeared to have a plausible excuse for every crime charged against him, except, perhaps, the killing of Carlyle. I said to him one day, "Billy, I pass no opinion as to whether your sentence is just for the killing of Brady, but had you been acquitted on that charge, you would most surely have been hung for the murder of Jimmie Carlyle, and I would have pronounced that sentence just. That was the most detestable crime ever charged against you." He seemed abashed and dejected, and only remarked, "There's more about that than people know of." In our conversations, he would sometimes seem on the point of opening his heart, either in confession or justification; but it always ended in an unspoken intimation that it would all be of no avail, as no one would give him credence and he scorned to beg for sympathy. He expressed no enmity toward me for having been the instrument through which he was. brought to justice but evinced respect and confidence in me, acknowledging that I had only done my duty without malice and had treated him with marked leniency and kindness.

As to his guards, he placed great confidence in Bell and appeared to take a great liking to him. Bell had been in no manner connected with the Lincoln County War and had no animosity or old grudge against the Kid. Although the natural detestation of an honest and law-abiding citizen like Bell for a well-known violator of the law was intensified in this instance by the murder of Carlyle, who was a friend of Bell's, yet never, by word or action, did he betray any prejudice or dislike. As to Ollinger, the case was altogether different. He and the Kid had met opposed in arms frequently during the past years of anarchy. Bob Beckwith, the bosom friend of Ollinger, had been killed by the Kid at the close of the

Billy the Kid

three days' fight in Lincoln. The Kid likewise charged Ollinger with the killing of friends of his. Between these two there existed a reciprocal hatred and neither attempted to disguise or conceal his antipathy from the other.

NOTE A

The Kid always appreciated the way Garrett stood by his promise to see the group of prisoners safely to Santa Fe. In talking with J. P. Meadows about the incident of the Las Vegas mob and Garrett's offer to put a six shooter in the Kid's hand if there was need, the Kid said, "I sure wanted to smell powder once more before I died."

He then went on to say of Garrett, "Pat Garrett is as white a man as ever stood in two shoes on God's earth. If I was laying out in an arroyo, and Garrett passed me and didn't see me, I'd be the last man to hurt a hair of his head. But if he saw me, I'd go to shooting and doing it fast."

When Meadows asked, "Kid, why do you feel that way?", the Kid replied, "Because he stuck to us so close in Las Vegas."

NOTE B

The Kid and Wilson were taken from Santa Fe to Mesilla by Tony Neis, deputy United States marshal, and Francisco Chavez, chief of police at Santa Fe. The journey was by train, and precaution was taken to offset any attempt at rescue by the Kid's friends or at lynching by his enemies. At Rincon, where the party had to change to the train for Mesilla, a threatening mob had gathered, but Neis and Chavez were able to stand them off. It is not certain whether the mob was friendly or hostile to the Kid.

NOTE C

Garrett's statement that the Kid was acquitted in Federal Court for the killing of Roberts is in accord with an impression that has had wide currency. But is not in agreement with the records of the United States district court. These show that the Kid's counsel, Judge Ira E. Leonard, was astute enough to raise the question of whether the Federal authorities had jurisdiction in this killing. Although it was commonly said that Roberts had been killed on the Indian Reservation, yet he had not been killed on land belonging to the United States Government. Dr. Blazer's house and other properties were on land to which he had acquired title before the establishing of the Reservation. When the Reservation was made, he and a few others who had obtained titles to their land remained in undisturbed possession of it.

Judge Bristol sustained the motion of Judge Leonard denying the jurisdiction of the Federal Court and quashed the indictment on April 6th, 1881. He, however, directed the United States marshal to deliver the Kid into the custody of the Territorial authorities to stand trial for the killing of Brady.

The Kid's trial in the Territorial court began on April 8th. By appointment of the court the Kid's attorneys were John D. Bail and A. J. Fountain, both of Mesilla. The prosecution was conducted by S. B. Newcomb, the district attorney. The first day was largely occupied with selecting a jury, both the prosecution and the defense using all privileges of challenge. Finally a jury was selected composed altogether of Mexicans. The jurymen were: Refugio Bernal, Jesus Telles, Felipe Lopez, Merced Lucero, Pedro Serna, Pedro Martinez, Crecencio Bustillos, Louis Sedillos, Pedro Onopo, Jesus Silva, Hilerio Moreno, Benito Montoya.

After the jury was empanelled, the taking of testimony was begun, the witnesses under subpoena being the following from Lincoln County: Isaac Ellis, J. B. Matthews, B. J. Baca, J. J. Dolan, Sam Corbett, and J. H. Blazer. The Kid had subpoenaed McCormick, Widermann and Ellis, but it is doubtful if all of these, especially Widermann, were present. The next day the jury finished hearing testimony, and completed their deliberations, bringing in a verdict of guilty. The other indictment pending in the Territorial court was nolle prossed.

Billy the Kid

Governor Wallace's version of his interview forms an interesting addition at this point. In June, 1902, General Wallace in an interview reported in one of the Indianapolis papers enlarged upon his reminiscences of his New Mexico experiences, and, from this account, when freed of its reporters' exaggerations and inaccuracies, the details of the meeting between the Governor and young outlaw can be reconstructed.

General Wallace went on to say that he wanted the Kid to testify to what he knew of the Chapman murder. So he arranged through a note deposited with one of the Kid's friends for a meeting at night in Lincoln. The Kid arrived punctually, and, in response to the knock on the door of Squire Wilson's small adobe house, the Governor called out, "Come in." The door opened, and there stood the Kid, his Winchester in his right hand, his revolver in his left. The Governor noted his slender figure, with a stoop to the shoulders, the narrow face, with the mouth that seemed always in a smile.

"I was sent to meet the Governor here at nine o'clock," said the Kid, in his rather effeminate voice. "Is he here?"

The Governor rose to his feet and held out his hand, inviting the visitor to a seat for the conference.

"Your note gave promise of absolute protection," said the young outlaw, warily.

"I have been true to my promise," replied the Governor. "This man," pointing to Squire Wilson, "and myself are the only persons present."

The Kid then lowered his rifle and returned his revolver to its holster. When he had taken a seat, the Governor at once presented his proposal that the Kid should testify before the grand jury and also before the trial court regarding the killing of Chapman. At the close of the Governor's request, he made this offer: "I will let you go scot free, with a pardon in your pocket for all your own misdeeds."

The Kid remained silent for several minutes and then replied, "Governor, they would kill me if I would do what you ask."

197

"We can prevent that," said the Governor, and proceeded to unfold in more detail the scheme he had in mind. The Kid was to consent to a fake arrest. He was to be seized when he was asleep, and his capture was to have all the appearance of a genuine one. The Kid insisted on the right to pick the men who were to make the arrest and took care that none who had been showing strong animosity toward him were to be in the party. He also stipulated that during his confinement he was to be kept handcuffed in order to give the arrest still more the appearance of being a real one and perhaps to protect his professional reputation as a desperado.

This plan was carried out, and Kimbrell, the Sheriff, made the Kid his prisoner and brought him to Lincoln. The Governor allowed the Kid on one day to give a sort of public exhibition of his skill with the rifle and the revolver. After seeing the Kid's prowess with both weapons, the Governor complimented him, and asked, "Billy, isn't there some trick to that shooting? How do you do it?"

"Well, General," replied the Kid, "there is a trick to it. When I was a boy, I noticed a man in pointing to anything he wished observed would use his index finger. With long use, the man unconsciously had learned to point with it with exact aim. When I lift my revolver, I say to myself, 'Point with your finger.' I stretch my finger along the barrel, and, unconsciously, it makes the aim certain. There is no failure; I pull the trigger and the bullet goes through to its mark."

General Wallace went on to tell of the Kid's escape from custody. One morning he said to his guards, "Boys, I am tired. Tell the General I am tired." With that he slipped his handcuffs from his wrists, walked out of the jail and over across the street, threw himself into the saddle on the back of a horse standing there, and dashed away in broad daylight, with no one to interfere.

General Wallace closed the interview with his version of the Kid's appeal to him, when he was later under arrest and realized his desperate straits. He sent word to the Governor that he would like to see him, but the Governor made no response to the request. Then the Kid sent the following note:

Billy the Kid

"Come to the jail; I have some papers you would not want to see displayed." Knowing that the Kid referred to the note he had sent about the meeting at Squire Wilson's, General Wallace proceeded to forestall such a move on the Kid's part by giving the newspapers a copy of the letter, accompanied by a narrative of the circumstances. When all this was published, the General had a copy sent to the Kid, and, according to Wallace's account, the latter had nothing further to say.

CHAPTER XXII

The Most Dramatic of All the Kid's Escapes—Killing of His Two Guards, Bell and Ollinger—His Get-away and Subsequent Movements.

ON the evening of April 28, 1881, Ollinger took all the other prisoners across the street to supper, leaving Bell in charge of the Kid in the guard-room. We have only the Kid's story and the sparse information elicited from Mr. Geiss, a German employed about the building, to determine the facts in regard to events immediately following Ollinger's departure. From all the circumstances and indications, the information from Geiss and the Kid's own admissions, the conclusions seemed to be as follows:

At the Kid's request, Bell accompanied him downstairs and into the back corral where was the jail latrine. As they returned, Bell, who was inclined to be rather easy-going in his guarding of the Kid, allowed the latter to get considerably in advance. As the Kid turned on the landing of the stairs he was hidden from Bell, and being very light and active, he bounded up the stairs, turned to the right, pushed open with his shoulder the door of the room used as an armory, which, though locked, was easily opened by a firm push, entered the room, seized a six-shooter, and returned to the head of the stairs just as Bell faced him on the landing of the staircase and some twelve steps beneath. The Kid fired, and Bell, turning, ran out into the corral in the direction of the little gate, but he fell dead before reaching it. The Kid ran to the window at the south end of the hall, from which he saw Bell fall; then slipping his handcuffs over his hands he threw them at the body, saying, "Here, damn you, take these, too." He then ran to my office and got a double-barrel shotgun. This gun was a very fine one, a breech-loader, and belonged to Ollinger. He had that morning loaded it in the presence of the Kid, putting eighteen buckshot in each barrel, and had remarked, "The man that gets one of these loads will feel it." The Kid then went from my office into the guard-room and stationed himself at the east window which opened on the yard.

Ollinger heard the shot and started back across the street, accompanied by L. M. Clements. Ollinger entered the gate leading into the yard just as Geiss appeared at the little corral gate and said, "Bob, the Kid has just killed Bell." At the same instant the Kid's voice was heard from above, "Hello, old boy," said he. "Yes, and he has killed me too," exclaimed Ollinger, and thereupon fell dead with eighteen buckshot in his right shoulder, breast, and side. The Kid then left the guard-room, went through my office into the hall and passed out on to the balcony. From there he could see the body of Ollinger as it lay in the projecting corner of the yard near the gate. He took deliberate aim and fired the other barrel, the charge taking effect in nearly the same place as the first. Then breaking the gun across the railing of the balcony, he threw the pieces at Ollinger, saying, "Take it, damn you, you won't follow me any more with that gun."

He then returned to the back room and armed himself with a Winchester and two revolvers. He was still encumbered with his shackles, but hailing old man Geiss, he commanded him to bring a file. Geiss found one and threw it up to him in the window. The Kid then ordered the old man to saddle a horse belonging to Billy Burt, deputy clerk of the Probate Court, which was in the stable. While waiting for this to be done, the Kid went to a front window which commanded a view of the street, and seating himself there, began to file the shackles from one leg. Bob Brookshire came out on the street from the hotel opposite and started down towards the plaza. The Kid saw him going in that direction, and bringing his Winchester down on him shouted, "Go back, young fellow, go back. I don't want to hurt you, but I am fighting for my life. I don't want to see anybody leave that house."

In the meantime, old man Geiss was having trouble with the horse, which broke loose and ran around the corral and yard for awhile; but at last he brought him saddled to the front of the house. While this was going on, the Kid was running about all over the building, now on the porch, now watching from different windows. He danced about on the balcony, laughed and shouted as though he hadn't a care on earth. He remained at the house for nearly an hour after the two killings before he made a motion to leave. When he left the house and attempted to mount the horse, the animal again broke loose and ran down towards the Rio Bonito. The Kid thereupon called to Andrew Nimley, one of the prisoners who was standing by, to go and catch it. Nimley hesitated, but a quick and imperative gesture by the Kid started him. He brought the horse back, and the Kid remarked, "Old fellow, if you hadn't gone for this horse, I would have killed you." This time the Kid succeeded in mounting, and saying to those within hearing, "Tell Billy Burt I will send his horse back to him," he galloped away, the shackles still hanging to one leg. He was armed with a Winchester and two revolvers. He took the road west leading to Fort Stanton, turned north about four miles from town, and rode in the direction of Las Tablas.

In order to understand all that happened it is necessary to go back a little in the story of this tragedy. It was found that Bell was hit under the right arm, the ball passing through the body and going out under the left arm. On examination it was evident that the Kid had made what was for him a very poor shot, and that his hitting Bell at all was a lucky accident. The ball had hit the wall on Bell's right, then caromed, and passed through his body, and buried itself in the adobe wall on his left. There were other proofs besides the marks in the wall that showed that this was the course of the bullet. The ball had surely been indented and creased before it entered Bell's body, as the grooves and crumplings on it were filled with flesh. The Kid afterwards told Pete Maxwell that Bell shot at him twice and just missed him, but there is no doubt that this statement was false. One other shot was heard before Ollinger appeared on the scene, but it is believed that it was an accidental one fired by the Kid while he was fooling with the arms in the armory. Ollinger was shot in the right shoulder,

GARRETT'S NOTATION ON THE KID'S DEATH WARRANT
TELLING OF HIS ESCAPE

Billy the Kid

breast, and side. He was literally riddled by thirty-six buckshot.

All the inhabitants of the town of Lincoln appeared to be terror-stricken. It is my firm belief that the Kid could have ridden up and down the plaza until dark without a shot being fired at him or any attempt made to arrest him. Sympathy for him might have actuated some of this, but most of the people were doubtless paralyzed with fear when it was whispered that the dreaded desperado, the Kid, had slain his guards and was at liberty again. To me the escape of the Kid was a most distressing calamity for which I do not hold myself guiltless. His escape and the murder of his two guards were the result of mismanagement and carelessness in great measure. I knew the desperate character of the man, that he was daring and unscrupulous, and that he would sacrifice the lives of a hundred men who stood between him and liberty, when the gallows stared him in the face, with as little compunction as he would kill a coyote.

And now I realized how inadequate all my precautions were. Yet, in self-defense and at the risk of being charged with shirking responsibility and laying it upon dead men's shoulders, I must say that my instructions as to caution and the routine of duty were not heeded and followed. On the bloody 28th of

April, I was at White Oaks, having left Lincoln on the day before to meet an engagement to receive taxes. I was at Las Tablas on the 27th and went from there to White Oaks. On the 29th I received a letter from John C. Delaney, the post trader at Fort Stanton, which merely stated the bare fact that the Kid had escaped and had killed his guards. On the same day Billy Nickey arrived from Lincoln and gave me further particulars. I returned to Lincoln on the 30th, and went out with some voluntary scouts to try and find the Kid's trail, but we were unsuccessful. A few days later Billy Burt's horse came in dragging a rope. This seemed to indicate the Kid had either turned him loose or sent him in by some friend who had brought him in to the vicinity of the town and headed him for home.

The next thing I heard about the Kid after his escape was that he had been at Las Tablas and there had stolen a horse from Andy Richardson. This horse he rode to within a few miles of Fort Sumner, but at that point the animal managed to get away from him, and the Kid walked into town with his presence unknown to anyone there. At Sumner he stole a horse from Montgomery Bell, who lived some fifty miles above, and who happened to be in town that day on business. This horse the Kid rode out

Billy the Kid

of town bareback, going in a southern direction. Bell, supposing the horse had been stolen by some Mexican, got Barney Mason and Mr. Curington to go with him to hunt it up. Bell left the others and went by himself down the Rio Pecos, while Mason and Curington took another direction, Mason carrying a rifle and six-shooter and Curington being unarmed. They came to a Mexican sheep camp, rode up close to it, and to their amazement the Kid stepped out and hailed them. Now the Kid had frequently designated Mason as an object of his direct vengeance; so on this sudden and unexpected appearance of the Kid Mason's business "laid rolling." He had "no sight on his gun," but he wore "a new pair of spurs." In short, Mason left. Curington remained, talked to the Kid, who admitted he had Bell's horse but said to tell Bell he was afoot and must have something to ride out of the country upon. He added that if he could make any arrangements he would send the horse back to Bell; if not, he would pay for it.

Subsequently to the Kid's interview with Curington he stayed for some time with one of Maxwell's sheep-herders about thirty-five miles east of Sumner. He spent some time also at various cow and sheep camps; and he was often at Cañaditas, Arenoso, and Fort Sumner. He was almost constantly on the move, living in this way about two and a half months and hovering in spite of danger around the scenes of his past two years of lawless adventure. He had many friends who were faithful to him, who harbored him, who kept him supplied with Territorial newspapers and other valuable information concerning his safety. His end had not yet come, but it was fast approaching.

Note A

Several accounts of the Kid's escape, all purporting to be derived from the Kid himself, exist among those who came into contact with him after his escape. One of the most reliable of these is that of J. P. Meadows, to whose place on the Penasco the Kid came a few days after leaving Lincoln. The Kid said that he had planned the attempt at escape very carefully, and on the particular day, when Ollinger had gone to supper, he saw his golden opportunity. He accordingly made the request of Bell that the latter conduct him to the outside, and the latter readily acquiesced.

As they were coming back, he got considerably ahead of Bell and after making the turn in the stairway, he took advantage of the rather long chain to his leg shackles to leap up to the top of the stairs. Then he quickly slipped his left hand free of the handcuffs, and when Bell came up the stairs, dealt him a blow over the head with the handcuffs. The Kid said that his intention was to stun Bell and make him a prisoner, then he proposed to arm himself and await the return of Ollinger. He planned to capture the latter and to handcuff him to Bell, but the Kid very frankly said that his final disposition of his enemy was to be shooting him in revenge for the long series of mistreatments and insults.

As the affair turned out, Bell started to run down the stairs, and the Kid, seeing the possibility of his giving an alarm, felt

Billy the Kid

forced to shoot him. In speaking of the matter afterwards to
J. P. Meadows the Kid regretted the necessity of doing
this, but added, "You see, I was fighting for my life, and
you know what a man will do under such circumstances."
He also said to Meadows anent the killing of Ollinger, "I
never felt so good in all my life as I did when I pulled trigger
and saw Ollinger fall to the ground."

The Authentic Life of

CHAPTER XXIII

Garrett Perfects Plans for the Kid's Recapture—The Fatal Shot in the Dark at Pete Maxwell's—The Kid's Burial in the Old Military Cemetery at Fort Sumner.

DURING the weeks following the Kid's escape, I was censured by some for my seeming unconcern and inactivity in the matter of his re-arrest. I was egotistical enough to think I knew my own business best, and preferred to accomplish this duty, if possible at all, in my own way. I was constantly but quietly at work seeking trustworthy information and maturing my plan of action. I did not show my face in the Kid's old haunts, nor did I disclose my intentions and doings to anyone. Most of the time I stayed at home and busied myself about the ranch. If my seeming unconcern deceived the people as well as gave the Kid confidence in his security, my end was accomplished. I was strongly inclined to believe that the Kid was still in the country and probably in the vicinity of Fort Sumner, yet there was some doubt mingled with this belief. The Kid had never been taken for a fool; on the contrary, he was generally credited with the possession of forethought and cool judgment in a de-

Billy the Kid

gree extraordinary for one of his age. It was therefore hard for me to believe that he would linger in the Territory in the face of all the elements in the situation—his liability to the extreme penalty of the law, the liberal reward for his detection and re-arrest, and the ease with which a successful flight into safety might be made. My first task was to resolve my doubts.

Early in July I received a reply to a letter I had written to Brazil. I was in Lincoln when the letter came to me, and Brazil was dodging and hiding from the Kid. He feared the latter's vengeance on account of the part he had taken in his capture at Stinking Spring. There were many others in that section of the Territory who trembled in their boots at the news of the Kid's escape; but most of them seemed able to talk him out of his resentment or to conciliate him in some manner. Brazil's letter gave me no positive information; he merely said he had not seen the Kid since his escape but, from many indications, believed he was still in the country. He offered me any assistance in his power in the recapture of the Kid. In reply to Brazil's letter I wrote and requested him to meet me at the mouth of Taiban Arroyo an hour after dark on the night of the 13th of July.

A gentleman named John W. Poe, who had super-

seded Frank Stewart in the employ of the stockmen
of the Canadian, was at the same time in Lincoln on
business, as was also one of my deputies, Thomas K.
McKinney. I first went to McKinney but did not
deem it wise to disclose to him my full intentions. So
I told him I wanted him to accompany me on a business trip to Arizona, but added that we would have to
go down to my home first and start from there. He
readily consented to this proposal. I then went to
Poe, and to him I disclosed my business and all its
particulars, even showing him the correspondence. He
also readily agreed to my request that he accompany
me on the expedition. We three then set out for
Roswell, and started up the Rio Pecos from there on
the night of July 10th. We rode mostly in the night,
followed no roads but took unfrequented routes, and
arrived at the mouth of Taiban Arroyo, five miles
south of Fort Sumner, about an hour after dark on the
night of the 13th. Brazil was not there. We waited
nearly two hours, but he did not come. We then rode
off a mile or two, staked our horses, and slept until
daylight. Early in the morning we rode up into
the hills and prospected a while with our field
glasses.

Poe was a stranger in the country, and there was
little danger he would meet anyone at Sumner who

THE MAXWELL HOME AT FORT SUMNER

The Maxwells had bought and converted into a home the southernmost of the two large buildings, west of the parade ground, which had been built for officers' quarters (see maps of Fort Sumner given earlier in this book). On the night when he was killed, the Kid came to a gate on the left-hand side of the picture, and went into the front corner room, which was Pete Maxwell's bedroom.

Billy the Kid

might know him. So, after an hour or two spent in the hills, I sent him into Fort Sumner to take observations. I advised him also to go on to Sunnyside, seven miles above Sumner, and interview M. Rudolph, in whose judgment and discretion I had great confidence. It was understood that Poe was to meet us that night at moonrise at La Punta de la Glorietta, four miles north of Fort Sumner. Poe went on up to the plaza, while McKinney and I rode down into the Pecos Valley, where we remained during the day. At night we started out circling around the town, and met Poe exactly on time at the trysting place. Poe's appearance, it seemed, had excited no particular notice, and he had gleaned no news there. When he went to Sunnyside and saw Rudolph, he learned that the latter was inclined to think from all indications that the Kid was about and yet at times he doubted if this were the case. The basis of this doubtfulness was not so much any actual evidence contradicting it, as his feeling that the Kid would not be fool enough, under the circumstances, to brave such danger.

When I had heard Poe's report, I concluded to go and have a talk with Pete Maxwell, in whom I felt sure I could rely. We three rode in that direction, but when we were within a short distance of Maxwell's place, we ran upon a man who was in camp. We stopped to see who it might be, and to Poe's great surprise, he found in the camper an old friend and former partner by the name of Jacobs, with whom he had been associated in Texas. So we unsaddled here and got some coffee. Then on foot Poe, McKinney, and I entered an orchard which ran from where we were down to a row of old buildings, some of which were occupied by Mexicans, not more than sixty yards from Maxwell's house.

We approached these houses cautiously, and when within ear-shot heard the voices of persons conversing in Spanish. We concealed ourselves quickly and listened, but the distance was too great to hear words or even to distinguish voices. Soon a man arose from the ground, close enough to be seen but too far away to be recognized. He wore a broad-brimmed hat, dark vest and pants, and was in his shirt sleeves. With a few words which reached our ears as merely an indistinct murmur, he went to the fence, jumped it, and walked down toward Maxwell's house. Little as we then suspected it, this man was the Kid. We learned subsequently that when he left his companions that night, he went to the house of a Mexican friend, pulled off his hat and boots, threw himself on a bed and commenced reading a newspaper. He soon, however, called to his friend, who was sleeping in the room, and told him to get up and make him some coffee, adding, "Give me a butcher knife, and I will go over to Pete's and get some beef. I'm hungry." The Mexican arose, handed him the knife, and the Kid, hatless and in his stocking feet, started to Maxwell's house, which was but a few steps distant.

When the Kid, who had been thus unrecognized by me, left the orchard, I motioned to my companions, and we cautiously retreated a short distance. In order to avoid the persons we had heard at the houses, we took another route, approaching Maxwell's house from the opposite direction. When we reached the porch in front of the building, I left Poe and McKinney at the end of the porch, and about twenty feet from the door of Pete's bedroom, while I myself entered it. It was nearly midnight and Pete was in bed. I walked to the head of the bed and sat down near the pillow and beside Maxwell's head. I asked him as to the whereabouts of the Kid. He replied that the Kid had certainly been about, but he did not know whether he had left or not. At that moment, a man sprang quickly into the door, and, looking back, called twice in Spanish, "*Quién es? Quién es?* (Who comes there?)" No one replied, and he came on into the room. I could see he was bareheaded, and from his tread I could perceive he was either barefooted or in his stocking feet. He held a revolver in his right hand and a butcher knife in his left.

He came directly towards where I was sitting at the head of Maxwell's bed. Before he reached the bed, I whispered, "Who is it, Pete?" but received no reply for a moment. It struck me that it might be Pete's brother-in-law, Manuel Abreu, who had seen Poe and McKinney on the outside and wanted to know their business. The intruder came close to me, leaned both hands on the bed, his right hand almost touching my knee, and asked in a low tone, "Who are they, Pete?" At the same instant Maxwell whispered to me, "That's him!"

Simultaneously the Kid must have seen or felt the presence of a third person at the head of the bed. He raised quickly his pistol—a self-cocker—within a foot of my breast. Retreating rapidly across the room, he cried, *"Quién es? Quién es?* (Who's that? Who's that?)" All this occurred more rapidly than it takes to tell it. As quick as possible I drew my revolver and fired, threw my body to one side, and fired again. The second shot was useless. The Kid fell dead at the first one. He never spoke. A struggle or two, a little strangling sound as he gasped for breath, and the Kid was with his many victims.

I went to the door, and met Poe and McKinney

there. Maxwell in the excitement had leaped over the foot of the bed, dragging the bedclothes with him; and now he rushed out the door past me and the others. Poe and McKinney threw their guns down on him, but he shouted to them, "Don't shoot, don't shoot." I told my companions I had got the Kid. They asked if I had not shot the wrong man. I told them I had made no mistake, for I knew the Kid's voice too well. To both of them the Kid was entirely unknown. They had seen him pass by them when they were sitting on the porch, and as he stepped up on it, McKinney, who had been sitting, rose to his feet. One of his spurs caught under the boards and nearly threw him. Observing this, the Kid laughed, but the next instant he probably saw their guns, and thereupon drew his own weapon as he sprang into the doorway, calling out, *"Quién es?"* Seeing a bareheaded, barefooted man, in his shirt sleeves, with a butcher knife in his hand, and hearing his hail in excellent Spanish, they naturally supposed him to be a Mexican and an attaché of the establishment; hence their suspicion that I had shot the wrong man.

We now entered the room and examined the body. The ball had struck him just above the heart and must have cut through all the ventricles. Poe asked me how many shots I had fired; I told him two, but stated that I had no idea where the second one went. Both Poe and McKinney said the Kid must have fired also, as there were surely three reports. I told them he had fired one shot, between my two. Maxwell also said that the Kid had fired once. Yet when we came to look for bullet marks none from his pistol could be found. We searched long and faithfully—found both my bullet marks but none other. So, against the impressions and senses of four men, we concluded that the Kid did not fire at all. We examined his pistol—a self-cocker, calibre 41. It had five cartridges and one shell in the chambers, the hammer resting on the shell. But this proved nothing, as many carry their revolvers in this way for safety. Moreover, the shell looked as though it had been shot some time before.

It will never be known whether the Kid recognized me or not. If he did, it was the first time during all his life of peril that he ever lost his presence of mind, or failed to shoot first and hesitate afterwards. He knew that a meeting with me meant surrender or fight. He had told several persons about Sumner that he bore no animosity against me and had no desire to do me injury. He had also said that he knew, should we meet, he would have to choose between the several alternatives of surrendering, or killing me, or getting

GRAVEYARD WHERE BILLY THE KID IS BURIED

Upper, gateway to what remains of the old military cemetery at Fort Sumner. *Lower,* approximate location of the Kid's unmarked grave, a short way south of the entrance. The man standing is Mr. Charlie Foor, an old resident of Fort Sumner, who remembers the location of the grave.

Billy the Kid

killed himself. So he had declared his intention in case we should meet to commence shooting on sight.

On the following morning, the alcalde, Alejandro Segura, held an inquest over the body, M. Rudolph of Sunnyside being foreman of the coroner's jury. Their verdict was that William H. Bonney came to his death from a gun-shot wound, the weapon being in the hands of Pat F. Garrett; and that the fatal wound was inflicted by the said Garrett in the discharge of his official duty as sheriff and that the homicide was justifiable. The Kid's body was neatly and properly dressed and buried in the old military cemetery at Fort Sumner, July 15, 1881. His exact age on the day of his death was twenty-one years, seven months and twenty-one days.

I have said that the body was buried in the cemetery at Fort Sumner. I wish to add that it is there to-day [1882] intact—skull, fingers, toes, bones, and every hair of the head that was buried with the body on that 15th of July, doctors, newspaper editors, and paragraphers to the contrary notwithstanding. Some presuming swindlers have claimed to have the Kid's skull on exhibition, or one of his fingers, or some other portion of his body, and one medical gentleman has persuaded credulous idiots that he has all the bones strung upon wires. It is possible that there is on exhibition somewhere in the States, or even possibly in this Territory, a skeleton which was procured somewhere down the Rio Pecos. We have them—lots of them—in this section. The banks of the Pecos from Fort Sumner to the Rio Grande are dotted with unmarked graves and the skeletons are of all sizes, ages, and complexions. Any showman of ghastly curiosities can resurrect one or all of them and place them on exhibition as the remains of Dick Turpin, Jack Sheppard, Cartouche, or the Kid, with no one to say him nay, so he does not ask the people of the Rio Pecos to believe it. Again I say that the Kid's body lies undisturbed in the grave, and I speak of what I know.

NOTE A

Poe's account of what happened at Pete Maxwell's on the night of July 14th, which was privately printed by E. A. Brininstool of Los Angeles, California, in 1923, is fuller in its details but is substantially the same as Garrett's. Poe adds to the account of Garrett's determination to seek the Kid at Fort Sumner the fact that Poe had learned that the Kid was hanging out at Fort Sumner through the confidential disclosures of an old acquaintance who had overheard in a livery stable at White Oaks a conversation between certain of the Kid's allies. Confident that the clue was worth following up, Poe looked up Garrett and laid the information before him. It was Poe's insistence that finally moved Garrett to make the trip to Fort Sumner.

NOTE B

An interesting supplement to the account of the death of the Kid is Garrett's official report to the Governor of New Mexico.

Billy the Kid

Governor Wallace had left the state, and the report was therefore made to acting Governor Ritch.

Fort Sumner, N. M., July 15, 1881.

To His Excellency, the Governor of New Mexico:

I have the honor to inform your Excellency that I have received several communications from persons in and about Fort Sumner, that William Bonny, alias the Kid, had been there, or in that vicinity for some time.

In view of these reports I deemed it my duty to go there, and ascertain if there was any truth in them or not, all the time doubting their accuracy; but on Monday, July 11, I left home, taking with me John W. Poe and T. L. McKinney, men in whose courage and sagacity I relied implicitly, and arrived just below Fort Sumner, on Wednesday 13th. I remained concealed near the house, until night, and then entered the fort about midnight, and went to Mr. P. Maxwell's room. I found him in bed, and had just commenced talking to him about the object of my visit at such an unusual hour, when a man entered the room in stockinged feet, with a pistol in one hand and a knife in the other. He came out and placed his hand on the bed just beside me, and in a low whisper, "Who is it?" (and repeated the question) he asked of Mr. Maxwell.

I at once recognized the man and knew he was the Kid, and reached behind me for my pistol, feeling almost certain of receiving a ball from his at the moment of doing so, as I felt sure he had now recognized me, but fortunately he drew back from the bed at noticing my movement, and, although he had his pistol pointed at my breast, he delayed to fire, and asked in Spanish *"Quién es? Quién es?"* This gave me time to bring mine to bear on him, and the moment I did so I pulled the trigger and he received his death wound, for the ball struck him in the left breast and pierced his heart. He never spoke, but died in a minute. It was my desire to have been able to take him alive, but his coming upon me so suddenly and unexpectedly leads me to believe that he had seen me enter the room, or had been informed by some one of the fact; and that he came there armed with pistol and knife expressly to kill me if he could. Under that impression I had no alternative but to kill him, or to suffer death at his hands.

I herewith annex a copy of the verdict rendered by the jury called in by the justice of the peace, (*ex officio* coroner) the original of which is in the hands of the prosecuting attorney of the first judicial district.

I am, Governor, very respectfully your Excellency's obedient servant,

Pat F. Garrett,
Sheriff of Lincoln County.

The verdict was given in Spanish in Garrett's report, its translation being:

We, the jury unanimously say that Wm. Bonney came to his death from a wound in the breast in the region of the heart, fired from a pistol in the hand of Pat F. Garrett, and our decision is that the action of the said Garrett was justifiable homicide; and are united in opinion that the gratitude of all the community is due to said Garrett for his action and that he deserves to be compensated.

(Signed) M. Rudolph, Foreman,
Antonio Saavedra,
Pedro Antonio Lucero,
José Silva,
Sabal Gutierrez,
Lorenzo Jaramillo.

Note C

In several accounts of the death of the Kid the statement is made that for the first time in his career he lost his presence of mind and so failed to shoot first. A moment's review of the situation will show, however, that the Kid must have done rapid and clear thinking in the circumstances confronting him. No sooner did he realize the presence of a suspicious stranger at the head of Maxwell's bed, than there must have flashed through

Billy the Kid

his mind that to shoot then might mean that he would kill his friend Maxwell. At the same instant almost must have come the recollection of the two men on the outside and the realization that they might attack him from the rear. So the Kid moved away toward the corner diagonally opposite to the one where was Maxwell's bed, in order to reach a position from which he might control the situation both as regards the stranger in the room and the two others on the outside. This decision, which clearly showed quickness of thought, involved a few seconds' delay, and of that delay Garrett took advantage under the impulse of the powerful law of self-preservation.

NOTE D

A few days after the killing of the Kid, Garrett in Santa Fe gave an interview to the *Daily New Mexican* in which he made an exoneration of Maxwell. He did not believe that Maxwell should be thought responsible for the presence of the Kid in his room on the night of his death. Maxwell, according to Garrett, was intimidated by the Kid's presence in the vicinity of Fort Sumner.

"How did the Kid happen to stop at Maxwell's house?" asked the reporter.

"He didn't stop there," replied Garrett. "He had only made three visits to Sumner since his escape and just came in unexpectedly while I was there. You see, I went to see Maxwell and ask him where Kid was. I asked him as soon as I got in whether Kid was in the country, and he became very much agitated, but answered that he was. Just then a man came in at the door and spoke to my men outside in Spanish, supposing them to be Mexicans. I didn't recognize him.

"He then came in and approached the bed, and after speaking to Maxwell, asked who were those outside. I had not had time to fix my revolver, and had not expected to see him there. I therefore reached around and adjusted it, and Maxwell started up in the bed. The Kid pulled down on me, and asked: 'Who is it?' He must have then recognized me, as I had him, for he went backward with a cat-like movement, and I jerked my gun and fired. The flash of the pistol blinded me, and I fired in the same direction again; and was ready to shoot the third time, but I heard him groan and knew that he was struck. All this, however, has been told. What I want you to say is that Maxwell was not guilty of harboring the Kid."

"I shall do that, but I want to ask you a few questions first. How do you account for the Kid not shooting as soon as he recognized you?"

"I think he was surprised and thrown off his guard. Almost any man would have been. Kid was as cool under trying circumstances as any man I ever saw. But he was so surprised and startled, that for a second he could not collect himself. Some men cannot recover their faculties for some time after such a shock. I think Kid would have done so in a second more, if he had had time."

"It is said by some people that Kid was cowardly, and never gave a man a chance."

"No, he was game. I saw him give a man one once. I have seen him tried. He would fight any way. I've known him to turn loose in a crowd of Mexicans, and get away with them. He would lick Mexicans that would weigh twenty-five or fifty pounds more than he did. He was quick as a flash."

"Was he a good shot?"

"Yes, but he was no better than the majority of men who are constantly handling and using six-shooters. He shot well, though, and he shot well under all circumstances, whether in danger or not."

"Why do you suppose he hung around Lincoln County?"

"Oh, he thought that was the safest plan. In fact, he said so. He said he was safer out on the plains, and could always get something to eat among the sheep herders. So he decided to take his chances out there where he was hard to get at."

Garrett's comment on the Kid's marksmanship may be disappointing to those who make him superlative in this respect,

Billy the Kid

but it is probably reliable and accords with the opinions of others who knew the Kid. Several of his crowd, Middleton for example, were considered much more expert with the pistol and the rifle than the Kid, but his most notable characteristic as a gunman was his coolness when engaged in any sort of shooting affray. It is said that he never showed the least excitement or discomposure.

ADDENDUM

THE life of the Kid is ended and my history thereof is finished. Perhaps, however, some of my readers will consent to follow me through three or four additional pages, which may be unnecessary and superfluous but which I insert for my own personal gratification, trusting that my friends will read them. While I was preparing this book for the press, some circumstances have occurred, some newspaper articles have appeared, and many remarks have been made, with reference to the disposal of the Kid, his character, disposition, and history, and my contemplated publication of his life, which I have resolved to notice against the advice of friends who believe the proper and more dignified plan would be to ignore them altogether. But I have something to say and propose to say it.

I have been portrayed in print and in illustrations as shooting the Kid from behind a bed, from under a bed, and from other places of concealment. After mature deliberation I have resolved that honest confession will serve my purpose better than prevarication. Hear, then. I was not behind the bed, because in the first place I could not get there. I am not "as wide as a church door," but the bed was so close to the wall that a lath could scarcely have been introduced between. I was not under the bed, and this fact will require a little more complicated explanation. I could have gotten under the bed; but, it must be remembered, I did not know the Kid was coming. He took me by surprise—gave me no chance on earth to hide myself. Had I suspected either his proximity or his coming upon me in that abrupt manner, I would have utilized any safe place of concealment which might have presented itself—under the bed or under any article I might have found under the bed big enough to cover me.

Some have claimed that I was scared on this occasion. Scared? Suppose a man of the Kid's noted gentle and amiable disposition and temper had warned you that, when you and he met, you had better "come a-shooting"; suppose he bounced in on you unexpectedly with a revolver in his hand while yours was in your scabbard? Scared? Wouldn't you have been scared? I didn't dare to answer his hail, "*Quién es?*" as the first sound of my voice, which he knew perfectly well, would have been his signal to make a target of me for his self-cocker from which he was wont to

Billy the Kid

pump a continuous stream of fire and lead in any direction unerringly as his will might dictate. Scared? Well, I should say so. I started out on that expedition with the expectation of getting scared; I went out contemplating the probability of being shot at and the possibility of being hurt, perhaps killed. But I did not intend to undergo such a catastrophe if precaution on my part would prevent it. The Kid really got a much better show than I had intended to give him.

Now about "the lucky shot," as they put it. It was not the shot but the opportunity that was lucky; and everybody may rest assured that I did not hesitate long about improving it. If there is anyone simple enough to imagine that I did then, or will ever, put my life squarely in the balance against that of the Kid or any of his ilk, let him divest his mind of that absurd fallacy. It has been said that "Garrett did not give the Kid a fair show," "did not fight him on the square," etc. Let me say that whenever I take a contract to fight a man "on the square" that man must bear the reputation, before the world and in my own estimation, of an honorable man and a respectable citizen, or, at least, he must be my equal in social standing; and I claim the right to place my own estimate upon my own character and to my own valuation upon my own life. If the public judges that these are to be measured by the same standard as those of outlaws and murderers whose lives are forfeit to the law, I beg the privilege of an appeal from its decision.

I had a hope—a very faint hope—of catching the Kid napping, as it were, and of being able to disarm and capture him. Failing in that, my design was to get the drop on him, for I believed he would make good his threat to "die fighting with a revolver at each ear." This would, of course, mean that, even with the drop in my favor, I would be forced to kill him. But at no time did I contemplate taking any chances which I could avoid by caution or cunning. The only circumstances under which we could have met on equal terms would have been accidental and involuntary on my part. Had such a meeting occurred unexpectedly, I have no idea that either of us would have run away, and then and there is where the "square fight" would doubtless have come off. With just one hypothetical question I will dismiss this subject of taking unfair advantage. What sort of "square fight" or "even show" would I have got, had one of the Kid's friends in Fort Sumner chanced to see me in Pete Maxwell's room that night and then had gone and informed the Kid of my presence there?

Finally, there have been some that took exception to

Billy the Kid

my writing and publishing a life of the Kid with the nefarious object of making money thereby. Their idea is that I must not attempt to make any more money out of the result of my "lucky shot." Anybody, everybody else, authors who were never in New Mexico and never saw the Kid, can compile from newspaper rumors as many lives of him as they please, make all the money out of their bogus, unreliable heroics that can be extorted from a gullible public, and these fellows will be congratulated. But my truthful history should be suppressed because I got paid for ridding the country of a criminal. How do these impertinent intermeddlers know how much money I have made by this accident, or incident, or whatever name they choose to designate it? How do they know how much it cost me to achieve the accident? How do they know how many thousands of dollars worth of stock and other property I have saved to those who rewarded me by my achievement? Whose business if I choose to publish a hundred books, and make money out of them all?

It is amusing to notice how brave some of the Kid's "ancient enemies," and even some who professed to be his friends, have become since there is no danger of their courage being put to the test by an interview with him. Some of them say that the Kid was a

coward—which is a cowardly lie—and anybody with
any nerve could have arrested him without trouble,
thus obviating the necessity for killing him. One has
seen him slapped in the face when he had a revolver
in hand without his resenting the insult. One has seen
a Mexican over on the Rio Grande choke him against
the wall, the Kid crying and begging with a cocked
pistol in his hand. These blowers are unworthy of
notice. Most of them were vagabonds who had
flopped from one faction to the other during the Lincoln County War, regulating their maneuvers according to the prospect of danger or safety, while
always keeping in view their chances to steal a sore-
backed pony or a speckled calf, and thus win the right
to be called stock-owners. There is not one of these
brave mouth-fighters who would have dared to give
voice to such lying bravado while the Kid lived, though
he had been chained in a cell; not one of them that,
were the Kid on his track, would not have set the
prairie on fire to get out of his reach. These silly
vaporings are but illustrations of that old fable, "The
Dead Lion and the Live Ass."

I will now take leave of all those of my readers who
have not already taken French leave of me. Whatever may be the cause back of the effect, Lincoln
County now enjoys a season of peace and prosperity

Billy the Kid

to which she has heretofore been a stranger. No Indians and no desperadoes appear on the scene to scare our citizens from their labors or to disturb their slumbers. Stock wanders over the range in security, and fields of waving grain greet the eye.